Do you have aims and ambitions you would like to achieve in your life? Or do you just wish your luck would change and you could attract some abundance and happiness? Perhaps you sometimes feel there are blocks in the way of this success – maybe even put there unconsciously by you, yourself.

Here is an ancient oracle, completely modernized by Titania, which can help you to attract good fortune into your life. By throwing the enclosed three special coins in a sequence, whilst concentrating on your immediate wishes or problems, you will arrive at a forecast. This will offer you not only an accurate mirror of your life as it is at present, but also how you can act to improve your situation and bring greater good fortune in the future.

In addition, each one of us has a status at birth that affects our behaviour through life. By understanding our own personalities we can cease to put blocks in the way of the good fortune to which we aspire.

TITANIA HARDIE

Illustrations by Richard Rockwood

GOOD FORTUNE
and how to attract it

QUADRILLE

CONTENTS

Introducing the oracle of Good Fortune

This oracle is ancient in origin. Based on the Chinese *Book of Changes*, familiarly known as the *I Ching*, the intention of this oracle of Good Fortune is to capture the wonderful wisdom, humour and energy of the original, while updating it for modern Western use. We no longer live in a society that is ruled by agrarian rhythms, or the automatic prioritizing of the eldest sons of our society. And women are no longer, in the West at least, naturally yielding and docile, uneducated, or subservient to all men! This is a huge development from the time when the *I Ching* was written, and the images that provided the metaphors for life in the time of Confucius may permit an adapted significance today.

The *Book of Changes* was intended to reflect the idea that life is never static – that all things and all people move and alter. I hope you will find that this modern, Western interpretation of the original oracle retains its lucid perceptions, while allowing it to move forwards into a changed perspective. Cultures move; ideas alter; opinions of what is right and wrong are fluid, from one country to another, and certainly over time. Opportunities for personal growth, for wisdom, and for achievement have had a meteoric transformation. Yet many aspects of human response to the world, to pain and joy, remain inherently the same.

This book, the new oracle of Good Fortune, is quite different from other interpretations of the *I Ching*, because so many of the images drawn from each forecast have been redefined to keep pace with our 21st century Western cultural background. It is no longer wrong or undignified or even 'dangerous' for a woman to make progress in her own right, for her to have a voice in what she would like, to make her own decisions, or even for her to be strong in the house of her husband! This was taboo at the time the *Book of Changes* was originally written. So I respectfully beg liberty from the enlightened *I Ching* proponents of today to keep their own humour and tolerance with the altered applications of the pictures of 3000 years ago. Personally, I feel that it is time for women, in particular, to enjoy their new freedoms and to see the wise observations of the book in a shifting landscape. If there are fresh truths to come from re-examining old wisdom, let us do that. If the book is truly a *Book of Changes*, it can embrace the revisions.

I have made much more use in this modern interpretation of the symbolic connections of the elements that make up the oracle: these were based on eight entities from the natural world, the Sky, the Earth, Thunder, Wind, Fire, Water, Lake and Mountain. These natural symbols were always affiliated with individual members of the family: mother, father and each child. As we understand much more clearly today how important is our position in the family in which we are born, and how it may affect us, I have elaborated on this facet of the oracle, and hopefully extended its interest and its applications for us individually. It is a fascinating journey. Once you have read about your personality type, based on your birth order, you can carry this information into the forecasts, knowing that certain forecasts – which include your element within them – are going to be of even more significance for you. I will talk more about this in the section beginning on page 8 on Personality Profiles.

Poetry is the first love of my life; and it was the poetic imagery of the *Book of Changes* that attracted me so powerfully in my teens. My first spiritual readings were with these pages, and I learned from this book long before I read my first professional tarot. With passing time, the book sheds new light. Always, it offers a perspective that helps us to negotiate any troubling situation: always, it suggests approaches to offset difficulties and turn defeats into victories with an altered attitude. It offers us, above all, a role as architects of our own good fortune!

Titania Hardie

How to attract good fortune

Decide where you are headed, and what your fate will be. Most importantly, aim higher. The oracle of Good Fortune will show you how to hurdle over obstacles that are inhibiting your success – they may only be in your mind!

In love, or career; with friends and in business; spiritually, materially, and emotionally – the oracle reveals your future to you, with clarity and detail. In addition, it offers wisdom and objectivity about how to rise to challenges in your immediate future and come out of every test successfully, feeling that you are in control.

Consulting the oracle, and understanding your Personality Profile, will allow you to see yourself differently, and to win at the game of life, rather than just survive! To win, the scales of the balance must tip much more towards laughter and happiness than towards dignity and poise. Laughter, and 'winning', will become an infectious and pleasant habit; you will raise your expectations in life, and ponder where you're headed. This applies in a material sense, but also in an emotional and personal sense. This is about feeling that you are the best you that you can possibly be, and it may meaning throwing off the shackles of how other people have traditionally judged you, or starting again with a new book of rules, this time written by you.

Choosing your future

The oracle is principally a philosophical treatise that offers an objective viewpoint in times of trouble. It definitely predicts the future, but you will discover that your future is not written in stone. It is for you to choose the details of your personal life story, effectively attracting your own fortune, and ensuring that it is good fortune.

The oracle's fusion of philosophy and fortune-telling explains the dynamics we create as individuals – in terms of our personality and our private interaction with the natural world – at any given time. Our identity, including our willingness to accept or challenge the role others see us fitted for, is understood to determine our fate: this is the idea that 'character is fate'. The oracle was originally conceived in the ancient world and in a very different society, but few modern psychologists or social historians would disagree that we are all, to a greater or lesser degree, culturally and emotionally affected by our relationships with our parents and siblings, and whether we are only children, or one of many. Even as adults, we often define ourselves as others perceive us. Our sensitivities and freedoms, our feelings of inner security, our selfishness or self-sacrificing tendencies, can all be understood to derive largely from this start in our lives, regardless of whether our upbringing was 'richer' or 'poorer' than someone else's.

The oracle is also concerned with our response to the seasons of the year. Whether we react with childish delight and enthusiasm to the sun or the snow, or whether we fold inwards and 'melt' in the heat or hibernate in the darkest winter days, is subjective. One way to understand our personal rhythms is to recognize how we are affected by the seasons, and in particular the one in which we were born. This, too, has a huge impact on our psychological and mystical states of being.

Find your personality type

The oracle of Good Fortune is concerned with our own presence on this planet – with the interactions we make with nature and the elements. When the moon shines on a perfect starlit night, we are affected. When the seas are stormy, we may reflect them. But these images are also metaphors for how we are as individuals at any given moment.

On pages 10–43, we look at these Personality Profiles, which are drawn from nature, determined by our order of birth and by our additional roles if we are parents. Understanding your individual Personality Profile will enable you to understand how you yourself have been understood, and what signals you give off to others. Have you subconsciously assumed the mantle of being a particular kind of person, of defined talents and expectations, perhaps according to how your parents described you? An awareness of this may enable you to slough away attitudes that have hindered greater personal fulfilment. It is a form of clearing away emotional blockages.

You are invited to relish the facets of your family life that are supportive and advantageous, and challenge and reject those that hold you back. You can vividly imagine

– and create – a different, brighter, happier future for yourself. In all things in life, I believe that whether you think you can or think you cannot do something, you're right! It starts right there in the architectural headquarters of your mind.

Your place in your family of birth

So let us start with the role you were born with. Let us consider what has influenced your personality, then we can understand some of its aspirations, and also its greatest challenges. What are your inclinations? What are your inherent responses to the world around you? Which symbols, drawn from the elements, are useful symbols for your awareness, and which are illuminating metaphors for your being?

Each Personality Profile is symbolized by an element taken from nature: the Sky, the Earth, Thunder, Wind, Fire, Water, Lake, and Mountain. On page 10 there is a chart that will show you your symbol, depending on your immediate birth position in the family. Your position in the family is determined by your relationship to your mother. Your parents' marriage may not have been their first, you may be the child of their first or one of their subsequent marriages, and you may have step-brothers and sisters. However, it is your mother who determines your emotional birth order, whether you are her first born or second born daughter or son, and so on. If you are a twin, one of you is still the elder, slightly. If you are a fourth daughter, or even a fifth, and if you are a fourth, fifth, seventh or even tenth son, you count on the chart as the third (and subsequent) son or daughter.

If you were adopted, you may have two separate roles. If you know the position you were to your birth mother, this counts. If not, count only your position in your adoptive family. In either case, if you do know your position to your birth mother, you will have two roles, but your principal role is the one in which you grow up, in the family who raised you.

If you are a parent, you have two concurrent roles. If you have children of your own (even if they are adopted), you will be either Earth (mother) or Sky (father), in addition to your position of son or daughter in your own birth family. Every mother will be Earth, as well as whatever position she holds in the family she was born into. Every father will be

Sky, and the same will be true. In fact, once you are a parent, the title of mother or father becomes more important and takes precedence, as it is the person you grow to become, and shows change and (hopefully) maturity. However, you are always somebody's son or daughter, even when one or both parents are dead, so this becomes a second part of your identity and is very illuminating.

Consult the chart on page 9 to see which element is synonymous with your birth order, and pages 10–11 to find which season you belong to according to your birth date. Then, read the description for your Personality Profile. Look at your potentials and strengths, and then consider your challenges. You will see then that you have a choice as to whether to live as the 'superior' man (as the ancient oracle would have said) and fulfil your positive qualities, or whether to lapse into negative traits. Of course we all do this sometimes, but the challenge is to fulfil the best opportunities, and by doing so, to attract good fortune to you.

Your Personality Profile

To find your Personality Profile symbol, identify yourself in relation to your mother. Were you her first, second, third or subsequent daughter or son (no matter how many fathers were involved)? You will see from the chart below which symbol fits your position. In addition, if you are a mother you are also Earth; if you are a father, you are also Sky. Then look at the chart on pages 10–11 to see the season you relate to most closely.

 First daughter: *WIND*

 First son: *THUNDER*

 Second daughter: *FIRE*

 Second son: *WATER*

 Third daughter: *LAKE*

 Third son: *MOUNTAIN*

 All further daughters: *LAKE*

 All further sons: *MOUNTAIN*

 Mother: *EARTH*

 Father: *SKY*

BORN DECEMBER 22nd – MARCH 21st

	in Northern Hemisphere	in Southern Hemisphere
First daughter	Winter wind	Summer wind
Second daughter	Winter fire	Summer fire
Third (and further) daughter	Winter lake	Summer lake
...and a mother	Winter earth	Summer earth
First son	Winter thunder	Summer thunder
Second son	Winter water	Summer water
Third (and further) son	Winter mountain	Summer mountain
...and a father	Winter sky	Summer sky

BORN MARCH 22nd – JUNE 21st

	in Northern Hemisphere	in Southern Hemisphere
First daughter	Spring wind	Autumn wind
Second daughter	Spring fire	Autumn fire
Third (and further) daughter	Spring lake	Autumn lake
...and a mother	Spring earth	Autumn earth
First son	Spring thunder	Autumn thunder
Second son	Spring water	Autumn water
Third (and further) son	Spring mountain	Autumn mountain
...and a father	Spring sky	Autumn sky

BORN JUNE 22nd – SEPTEMBER 21st

	in Northern Hemisphere	in Southern Hemisphere
First daughter	Summer wind	Winter wind
Second daughter	Summer fire	Winter fire
Third (and further) daughter	Summer lake	Winter lake
...and a mother	Summer earth	Winter earth
First son	Summer thunder	Winter thunder
Second son	Summer water	Winter water
Third (and further) son	Summer mountain	Winter mountain
...and a father	Summer sky	Winter sky

BORN SEPTEMBER 22nd – DECEMBER 21st

	in Northern Hemisphere	in Southern Hemisphere
First daughter	Autumn wind	Spring wind
Second daughter	Autumn fire	Spring fire
Third (and further) daughter	Autumn lake	Spring lake
...and a mother	Autumn earth	Spring earth
First son	Autumn thunder	Spring thunder
Second son	Autumn water	Spring water
Third (and further) son	Autumn mountain	Spring mountain
...and a father	Autumn sky	Spring sky

WIND

All eldest daughters of all seasons

The wind is inspirational and energetic, whipping up inert situations. A force unto itself, it is refreshing and recharging, searching and restless, exploring places where others rarely follow. Wind plays with us: teases our hair, challenges our complacency, asks us to be resourceful and strong in a crisis. It is moody: a gale when angry, a breeze when flirtatious. The wind laughs over the sea, embracing the trees on shore; it looms over deserts, rippling the sand and hypnotizing our vision. It drifts the snow, altering the landscape and challenging the world we perceive. A bridge between heaven and earth, the wind sets out to achieve – to progress the seasons and awaken the life force in all.

Wind's potential You may aspire to lead, to be admired, to be impressive when it is required, and to stand out from the crowd. You can be teasing and gentle, or forceful and dynamic. You are ambitious in a positive way – determined to move onward and upward, and to have fun and learn while you are doing it. With artistic flair and the will to find new ways of doing things, you are confident, passionate and sensuous, with high ideals and an aesthetic nature. You strive for perfection and self-fulfilment, seek self-improvement, and want to beautify yourself and your surroundings. You are friendly and successful. Love blossoms from you when you are feeling abundant, at which times you are desirable and tactile. Wind, the eldest daughter, does not feel inferior to any man.

Wind's challenges A lack of energy, or scope for self-expression, can lead to disloyalty or shallowness. You may put too much emphasis on appearances. If you feel unappreciated, you can become deceptive and misleading. If thwarted, you can become underhanded; if misunderstood, you can become envious and frustrated. When gentleness fails to bring the results you desire, a storm will erupt and you will be unreachable until your wrath has subsided. Beware of a tendency to insensitivity, and a difficulty in loving and being loved.

WINTER WIND: Keyword – Strength

You are bountiful, wise and strong. With profound emotional depth and the capacity to draw out the best in many people, you nevertheless keep your own feelings closely guarded, expressing yourself through metaphor or in the abstract. You are down to earth, up-front, and less frivolous than your sisters. You are selfless in extraordinary moments, able to help others who have lost their way, caring even for strangers. You may be attracted by dramas, too, and work in situations requiring spontaneous responses to difficulties. Your life is rarely uneventful. But when you feel a lack of hope within any situation, your heart becomes heavy and you retreat into a dark mood. You may become irritable and confused, frustrated, tense, and even speak loudly without your calm authority. Though usually forgiving, if you felt you were unheard in childhood, or that your dreams were ridiculed by loved ones, you can become indifferent and resentful. Then you may exchange your inner powers of determination for angry outbursts, which may be aimed at anyone near you. Try to prevent this build-up of nerves and temper, and keep a cool head.

SPRING WIND: Keyword – Trusting

You are a forgiving and trusting soul, with a good nature and faith in people. Flirtatious and vibrant, you create beauty around you, soothe away pains and apathy in others, and take trouble over details with friends and in business. You are mindful of other people's feelings and worries, and instinctively feel that good will always triumph over evil. This sometimes, inevitably, leads to disappointment; but, though you are at times taken advantage of, your buoyant cheerfulness more often leads you to fall on your feet and create serendipitous events around you. Innocent, and at times even naïve, you must be careful about betraying other people's secrets, which they will always tell you. Try not to waste your emotions on people who cannot return your spirited feelings. You must also be careful of tension and stress, which comes from having such a feminine, open personality. You are intuitive and sensitive, but you do need room to breathe without interference; you must build up your physical strength, and find ways to manage the stresses that sometimes swamp you.

SUMMER WIND: Keyword – Welcoming

You would willingly fill the days of all around you with love and the promise of joy; you have a childlike innocence and trust in people, yet you can also be the classic temptress, with a radiant energy that is nurturing of others. With a powerful imagination and bright and diverse ideas, your head is full of flowers, trees and angels. And while you can be almost fairy-like, you also have a dry, witty sense of humour that makes you lots of fun. You may love the sensuous things in life – beautiful clothes, good food and drink; but laughter with friends is an even stronger tonic, and for you, long, merry evenings are the best remedy for the stresses and strains of everyday life. Primarily a gentle soul, who doesn't always fully grasp the machinations of others, you may dream too much. You would never hurt another person but, if you are in a negative frame of mind, you might run the risk of being self-destructive and depressed. You must not give too much of yourself away. You may end up burnt-out as a result of worrying too much about what you should do with your life. On form, however, you are full of laughter and love.

AUTUMN WIND: Keyword – Compassion

You have a surprising serenity for someone who is both alert and prone to change. You are happy to mother people who need your time and care; but you also have an intriguing element of male strength – a true balance of feminine and masculine. You are gentle, wise and kind, but also strong, perceptive, direct and alert. You may need to overcome obstacles in your life; you also make sacrifices for others, coming to the rescue when friends are in trouble. Life may not always be smooth, and this is because you think deeply, and injustices upset you. You are versatile, sometimes given to flights of fancy, but can be tense, and may refuse to share your own problems freely enough. This can lead to exhaustion due to an inability to rest properly. Gentle and intelligent, you must let go of your own stresses and fight a tendency to obsessive behaviour. Maybe you feel a lost inner child in you, or a doubt about self-perfection? You may hold yourself back eternally if you worry constantly about making mistakes. Look to your amazing strengths of visual clarity and spirituality to overcome emotional conflicts and nervous illnesses. Practical and sensible, you can draw huge reservoirs of strength from the earth and nature.

FIRE

All second daughters

Radiant, warming, illuminating, brilliant, Fire is the spirit of the sun – warmth to share with family and friends, social and expressive, an essential source of comfort in our lives. As a means of cooking, it is the cornerstone of hospitality. As a lamp or candle, it dispels gloom, offering comfort and security. Turning our faces to the sun, we feel hope. With lightning, there is a sudden lucid flash before the storm, a strike of anger, a glow of passion: then the world is washed clean again. Fire's strength must not be underestimated.

Fire's potential When balanced and wise, you are lightness itself. Generous, warm-hearted, and optimistic, you comfort friends in distress and understand others' points of view, for there was always someone who came before you in the family so you are able to mediate. You see clearly and think positively – things will somehow always work out in the end. You are competitive, blazing brighter when Wind, your older sister, fans the flames! You have passion and gentleness, and are alive to everything. Erotic, vibrant, a sexy dancer rather than a ballerina, your inner glow will carry you through most crises. You soothe people's deep emotions, and can affect their souls. Artistic and poetic, you will enjoy work that gives you freedom. You are diplomatic, knowing how to bring people together.

Fire's challenges When you lose your balance and become defensive, or are provoked by jealousy and insecurity, you can be overbearing and deceptive. You may unwittingly become involved in power struggles, and your diplomatic skills may become manipulative. Worst of all, if you feel wronged or misunderstood, you can become destructively competitive and even vengeful – especially if somebody close to you is hurt. Be careful not to work too hard: you may become controlling, impatient, or even self-destructive. It is also a challenge to do what you can for people without having an 'I know best' attitude. But usually, you are enlightened and tolerant, bringing hope where there was none before.

WINTER FIRE: Keyword – Awakening

You bring laughter and light in the darkest moments, dazzling others when you need to inspire. Though you can spark up and become radiant in the right company, you can also be introverted and quiet. You have strong feelings about the spirituality of all things and the idea that there are aspects to heaven and earth we cannot see. Spiritually awakened, you are often quite fairy-like, with a high consciousness. You are cheeky, with a zany humour, and friendship is precious to you. You like new points of view and new places to explore; and you can leave people, problems and places behind under strictest need. Like sunshine in winter, which is often quite unexpected, you can often surprise people (and even yourself); but you must try to let go of past hurts. If you are still trying to discover who you are, spend time on this question: your self-enlightenment will, potentially, astonish you!

SPRING FIRE: Keyword – Purity

You are a true child of light. Spiritual, like your winter sister, you have an innate wisdom that takes you beyond worldly knowledge. You are the fiery sun returning in spring from its winter sleep, rising out of apathy. You remain ageless, enjoying everything in nature from the tiniest flower to the loftiest mountain. You have good intentions, which may sometimes be mistaken by others, but you usually don't bear grudges. You love seeking the mysteries of life, and despair at the intolerance of people in the world. You've a warm heart, enjoy fun with close friends, and need private time, too. You are good with children, clever with your hands at crafts and arts and even baking, and your sense of humour allows you to see the funny side of most things. Jealousy is occasionally a problem for you, but 'lightness' is your special strength.

SUMMER FIRE: Keyword – Spontaneous

You are a daring and quite hypnotic soul. Charming, good company, you must be careful not to reveal the secrets of those who feel compelled to confide in you. You enjoy danger, take some risks, but usually know where to draw the line. You can be obsessive, and you can become concerned about your appearance. Often extremely pretty, you know how to use your looks to get a reaction from others. You may be one of two types: summer lightning – quick on the uptake, and witty without trying, but also quick to flare at people if they wrong-foot you; or a lazy summer sun who exudes sensuality and expansiveness, but take care – this can wither into resentment and over-sensitivity. Or, you may be a little of both. But you do motivate people and help them see, by example, that absolutely anything is possible.

AUTUMN FIRE: Keyword – Patience

You know that some things are worth waiting for, and that this is required in life. You can be sweet, calm and very feminine, but you take no nonsense from anyone. Confident about who you are, you will pursue a goal in spite of any opposition; you love your home and family, and like to pamper those nearest to you. There are interesting emotional blocks from the past that need to be addressed eventually; but, once you confront this, your life will become quite structured and stable. You appreciate the transient moments in life, and sometimes enjoy a kind of gallows humour, wisely finding something that's good in every test. More of a parent than a lover, perhaps, you nevertheless flirt outrageously at times, not to catch someone else's man but because it's fun! You can be possessive and controlling, and you may be a drama queen on occasions. But you will trek on until a change comes, knowing that it will.

LAKE

All third (and subsequent) daughters

Joy is synonymous with Lake, the third daughter, the gift of the gods. She just is: loved, bringing pleasure, reflecting Father Sky in her face, cradled in the arms of Mother Earth. She may be spoiled by her family, but is less over-protected and duty-pledged than her sisters, Wind and Fire. The Lake is fed by the mountains and the sky, signifying a time of plenty and luxury. The reflection of all the seasons is mirrored in her beautiful face: she knows everyone in the family, reads them well, hears what they feel and sees what they see. Reflective and calm, her temper is less easily provoked than her siblings. Lake is more sheltered, reflects the world back to us, and mirrors our feelings with sensitivity. She is often a place of pleasure. She watches life with deep concentration.

Lake's potential Lakes are appealing and lovable. Steady and supportive, they are less ambitious in some ways than their sisters, but are still frequently risk takers. They love family history, cherish memories, keep the photo albums, and are good organizers. Neither extrovert nor introvert, Lakes like to feel secure and bond with other people, and they are faithful and dependable friends. They are creative, playful and a pleasure to be with. They may be conventional, but will speak out against authority with surprising warmth if it is behaving unfairly. They are endearing, dedicated and willing to please.

Lake's challenges If you were born late in your parents' lives, you may feel too heavily depended upon. Under stress, Lake's child-like spirit, normally so appealing, may become immature and full of inferiority complexes. If self-criticism and insecurity take hold, you could become masochistic and over-sensitive; you may also lose your common sense, becoming defensive and anxious. This may be the result of a limited range of possibilities offered to you. Then, the Lake becomes stagnant and lacks clarity. Try not to feel sorry for yourself, as this robs you of your otherwise excellent humour and imagination.

WINTER LAKE: Keyword – Purity

Though a child of the colder months, you are like a breath of fresh air in summer. Lively and positive, not bothered by the stresses and strains of daily life, you have energy and sparkle, like crisp water on a chilly, perfect day. You can be stimulatingly sweet or playfully sharp with friends, urging them to dip a toe in the bracing challenges of life; but you yourself only become interested in things you feel strongly about. If you enjoy your work you may become a workaholic; but when a business deal fades, you smile and go out for lunch, thinking ahead to the next thing. You find answers to life's questions, are rarely ill, and maintain a positive approach. When something really upsets you, you can become icy and distant; if you feel taken for granted you may become selfish and scattered, even absent minded. But a holiday will usually restore your joyful humour and liveliness.

SPRING LAKE: Keyword – Liberating

You have fantastic clarity and positivity about life and people, and you are finely attuned to other people's rhythms and feelings, like a mirror watching a blossoming world. You can somehow always approach life with freshness – no matter how many times you've seen and heard it before. You are happy and warm, brimming with energy even under testing circumstances, finding smiles to provoke and reflect back to your friends and loved ones. You love people and long to see them enjoy their full potential; in this, you are a good motivator. Exuding a gentle joyfulness, you can sing and laugh with no apparent self-consciousness. You feel people's innermost thoughts, though others don't always recognize this, seeing your buoyant exterior much more obviously. You are a clear thinker and healer, with the power to free yourself and others from past baggage. However, too much responsibility makes you nervous and irritable. Take time at a spa to rest and unwind when you need to.

SUMMER LAKE: Keyword – Happy

Few people can resist your company: you have a cheerfulness that survives all kinds of tests. You are open-hearted, witty and honest; less shy than the other Lake personalities, you have a way of knowing when someone needs a quick cuddle or a phone call. With your easy humour, friendly smile and sensuous nature, you seem to have the effect of a tonic on everyone around you. You will manage in any vocational path, but come alive when it is a job with people – publicity, management, show business, even charity work suits you perfectly. You are always able to tease someone out of a mood. Because you give so much, you are open to possible exploitation, which would make you depressed, even if you didn't own up to it for a while. Choose your life partner very carefully, as you must be able to trust them not to abuse your good nature. You'll be a good parent and stay philosophical under pressure, usually staying young and joyful for years. You have an inner radiance which helps you exude a beauty that's all your own.

AUTUMN LAKE: Keyword – Sympathetic

Your birth period is the time of change and preparation for the colder months ahead, but you are as sunny as your spring and summer Lake sisters. Perhaps a shade gentler and less bubbly, you are kind and loving with a good heart for all living creatures. You keep cards from friends and flowers pressed in pretty boxes; and the endearing child-like qualities you possess belie a sympathetic and astute understanding of other people and their problems. You will take on less fortunate people who need attention and a lift. You, too, need some looking after and protecting, but you can be quite a tough cookie too! Left to manage for yourself, you will get by admirably. You eat well, bloom in all seasons, and remain young. Sometimes, your real sunshine persona is a response to pain or sadness in your early life, mild gentleness having been a good way to cope. But people underestimate you if they ignore your strength. You're a risk taker, like all Lakes, and will question authority when pushed. Gentle, but assertive, you are full of surprises.

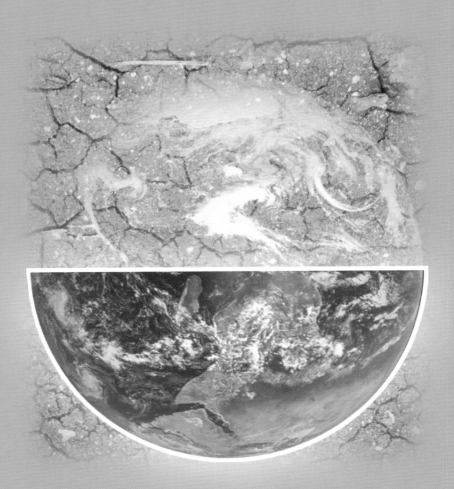

EARTH

All mothers of all seasons

The Earth springs anew every year with the gift of life. Rich, variable, humble and proud, the Earth is the womb from which life grows and to which life returns. Nurturing, surprising and unfathomable, it is our home and our truth. Colours change across the globe, with many influences making their mark: the Earth shelters every one of us. The perfect complement to the heavens, Earth is the sacred feminine principle, divine because she supports life and receives us all back to her without judgement. In winter, she appears to sleep; in summer, to teem; in spring, she pulses with new life; in autumn, she is enriched by ripe return to the ground. But the constancy of her love never changes, nor her need for respect and understanding from us. Earth is our grounding, our awareness of all things, the realm of our being.

Earth's potential Earth's aim is simple: to love, and to be loved, unconditionally. Earth needs to be appreciated and needed. Earth is receiving and empathetic, compassionate, welcoming and supportive. Earth people – mothers – give encouragement and are unselfish. Charitable, humanitarian and generous, Earth is the person who looks to be of help beyond call. Earth steps in to solve another person's crisis for them; she is honest and steady, reliable and kind, sympathetic and well-intentioned. She thinks naturally of others – not necessarily sacrificing her own needs, but working in a co-operative spirit.

Earth's challenges When taken for granted, Earths become martyrs. They seek sympathy, and acquire psychosomatic illness. They may feel that they do much for others, and yet are not noticed, and they can be smothering! They need to step back and address the challenge not to be so demanding and domineering at times: to allow others to be themselves, and not to assume that their good-natured 'interference' is always welcome. A saintly role has its drawbacks, and may give rise to the infliction of guilt on others.

WINTER EARTH: Keyword – Restorative

Everyone experiences sadness in the winter, except you! You are young at heart and understand the passage of time in a different way from most people. Imaginative and happy from an inner spring, you are patient and sensitive, with an ability to fortify yourself against the inevitable, understanding the true importance of life. Without some pain, you understand, joy would be less vivid. You have a refreshing approach to the problems of love and happiness, direction and aimlessness. Gentle but determined, you are free from mental limitations. You put things in order, and balance work and home better than many mothers. You are conscious of the earth's needs, are aware of what you eat, like growing things, and have many ideals. When stressed, you may become withdrawn, indecisive, and strained. If relationships disappoint your expectations, you may become temperamental and irritable. But your power is your sincerity and your amazing capacity to provide a safe haven for others in distress, a place for them to recover quietly.

SPRING EARTH: Keyword – Fostering

A bubbly personality with many interests, you are well organized and love life – every day is too precious for you to waste. You enthuse everyone you meet; you tantalize people with possibilities; yet you exude this constant stream of energy with a relaxed air – like a bubbling spring, rather than a torrent issuing from a waterfall. Your house is homely and cheerful. You know about health matters, and love to walk and enjoy the daylight. You take up new things, but with good judgement rather than frivolity. You need a partner in life who lives in the present tense with you: looking back over the past is a liberty you can't afford. You must refuse to let others lay emotional guilt on you, for this leads you to apathy and confusion. You are eager to press forward, always, and being forced to slow down for someone who wants you all to themselves is an impossible wrench. Jealousy and cynicism are sometimes aimed at you because you are such a free spirit; but you will defend yourself from this philosophically, looking for the best in everyone. Your playful personality, humour and cheerfulness help you through life's tests.

SUMMER EARTH: Keyword – Healing

Many things to many people: friendly, comforting, flexible. You gently mother those nearest to you, though you know how to allow people the freedom of their own thoughts, without interfering. You help others to feel secure, and offer a space for them to talk and unwind. You ease others' stresses by hearing them out, and happily care for your family. But you frequently take on too much, without making enough peaceful time for yourself. Steady, rather than eccentric, you still attract a group of individualistic friends who love your enthusiasm and lack of nonsense. Your home is often full of people, and your dinner table hosts a diverse group of friends. Don't end up doing too much for everyone without asking others to do their share! The generosity in your nature is open to exploitation. Try to shout for support sometimes, before your load becomes unbearable. Your strength is your humour and your ability to find tranquillity in trying circumstances; this counters your occasional irrationality or tendency to absorb anxieties. Look after your inner child; speak out gently before you reach a crisis.

AUTUMN EARTH: Keyword – Harmony

Though a child of the autumn, your character is full of sunshine and joy. You are gentle and peaceful, a person who can talk to angels and see colours when others see muted sepia. You calm and soothe people, and have an astonishing power to rally those who slip or feel weak. You commit yourself fully to what you believe in – half-hearted notions are not for you. You are good company, interesting to talk to, with myriad interests. Though you like to be appreciated, you are uncomfortable with overt praise. Sometimes, to recharge your battery, put a 'Do not disturb' sign on your door, allowing you time to digest what is happening to you or get on with your own important projects. You are dejected if someone deals you an injustice, or falsely accuses you of something unfair. Truly feminine, you often talk a great deal, but have a wonderful ability to bring balance to those around you.

THUNDER

All eldest sons

Thunder speaks and we all listen; his voice rises from the earth, calling to the heavens. Always expressing potential power, Thunder may be gentle, rumbling with energy and ideas, or angry, booming to the world. Thunder is decisive, strong-minded, and proud. His is a road of great potential; he must wander and gain experience, travelling everywhere, searching always. He is strong and emphatic, often spiritual, inspired by the gods. Like the eldest son poised to take over the power of his father, Thunder speaks of a coming storm. Much is expected from the eldest son; much is offered, too. His struggle is to find his own voice, his own power. Thunder tells us change is on the way. A cleansing prophet, he releases tension from the past, but must learn to express his emotions gently.

Thunder's potential Thunder is alive, strengthening those around him, daring the world to move forwards and change. He motivates his siblings, creating progress, washing away the stagnant past. He is eloquent, charismatic, and passionate. He has courage and fortitude. He can be a gentle giant, capable of power. Vivid and warm, he has a wicked sense of humour, is masculine and forceful, but sorts out problems philosophically. Not especially possessive, he likes the freedom to wander, and is both a good listener and communicator. Confidence radiates from him when he is focused and driven.

Thunder's challenges If he feels he is unheard, or if someone has been disloyal or disrespectful, his temper can erupt and he may demand the impossible from those closest to him. Thunder may guard his privacy jealously, and if he feels others have expectations he doesn't want to fulfil, his humour deserts him. He can hold a grudge a long time, and may see things as 'too black' or 'too white'. His is a sexual nature, but when depressed, he just withdraws into himself, sulking or bottling things up. Losing his purpose is the worst danger – he must keep active and interested in people and the world.

WINTER THUNDER: Keyword – Encouraging

More than any of your Thunder brothers, you are the strong silent type. You are stimulating and good company, encouraging to everyone – the world's favourite uncle. You let others do their thing, and expect to be left to do yours. Less of a talker than other Thunders, you are the best listener and would make a good counsellor, social worker or psychologist. You love finding new ways to do things – in your own time. Winter Thunder never rushes, but rumbles until it is ready. You love big spaces, especially in empty places. Be careful not to suffer in silence from emotional burn out; you will be unstable if you lose your direction or become unemployed. You have a good ability to bounce back, however, and can usually turn pangs of loneliness into appreciation of much needed quiet time.

SPRING THUNDER: Keyword – Motivating

Though born in springtime, you are an old soul. You have seen it before – watched changes and rearrangements in people's lives, and you somehow find the stamina to go through it again if necessary. Always at odds with your age, you may be 30 when you're 15, but 15 when you're 50! At work, you are stimulating to others, encouraging them to drive on and do well, complimenting as you go along. You like to be in charge, and find energy to tackle everything. You are good at law, understand documents, and speak up against unfairness. You are good to your friends, but family always comes first. With a rare but potentially fiery temper, you have huge charisma, but must be careful not to dictate to everyone, or to become entrenched in your views. Losing your direction is the worst danger, for when fatigued or disorientated, you become begrudging and emotionally cold. Keep smiling!

SUMMER THUNDER: Keyword – Fair-minded

You are a larger-than-life personality: affable, practical and intelligent with a big heart. You are both adventurous – loving to roam and see new faces and places – and yet quite conservative at times. You may often speak in favour of preserving customs and traditions, rather than breaking free from the old order. Both assertive and aggressive, you are fair to women, and don't think in quite the same terms as other people. You battle for your family and your home, protecting them vigorously; you run things smoothly and are admired by your peers and co-workers. You stand up for your rights, and expect standards from everyone. Nervous exhaustion is your worst fear – you sometimes overdo it and have to slow down. Also, fight mental stagnation by seeking new material to read or learn as you get older. But you are trustworthy and fair to everyone, hearing both sides of any argument.

AUTUMN THUNDER: Keyword – Clarity

You are straightforward and forthright: those who know you know what to expect. Without hidden motives or secret moves, you have good ideas and motivate others well. You are so enthusiastic about everything, but you must be careful not to weary others who can't keep up. You have the power to balance people around you, to find what's missing and fill it in. You're a good leader, you believe in justice for all, and you see things very clearly, speaking out passionately if you feel the need. Once aroused, your energy is committed; when your steam rises, you go for the throat! You will rescue those who are confused or lost, but you must watch your own levels of mental stress and stop them from rising out of control. Then you become judgemental and self-justifying, rigid and untrusting of all. Once you have screamed, though, your equilibrium usually returns.

WATER

All second sons

Water must be respected. Moisturizing and life sustaining, it can rise to dangerous levels and demand our caution, It seeks to fit in, to find its own level, to find a way through any terrain, slowly and patiently if necessary, drop by drop. As rain, it refreshes us, delights us, and sometimes drenches us. As the sea, it invites us to linger or explore, or it can truly terrify us. When we forget to pay it true heed, it is beyond our control and swallows us. Yet it bends and flows in the winding course of a river, and has the power to negotiate. Caressing, refreshing, chilling, silent or roaring, water has many moods according to our treatment. Never predictable, Water, the second son, may try to outdo Thunder, his elder brother, rising to overtake the other children, seeking identity, becoming competitive.

Water's potential If motivated, he will tenaciously find his way in life – sometimes rebellious, sometimes going with the flow. Less is expected of him than of Thunder – he makes less fuss, says less, but possibly quietly does more. He is easy-going but determined to get his share of attention, and has the ability to bring people together. When he is encouraged and richly fed, he strikes a silver path through the land, a ribbon reflecting the moon or the sun, the mother and the father. Able to hear everyone, to feel for everyone, to be quiet and to listen deeply, he has humour and persistence, and will explore the strangest places. Even the sweetest Water has hidden depths – and an excellent memory!

Water's challenges Water may become nervous and tense when things are not going his way, and a fear of failure and self doubts may obstruct his free expression. He can uncooperative and sulky if jealous; he is vulnerable to criticism, maybe with low self-esteem. If weary, he is stagnant like the water in a ditch, becoming unimaginative and sullen. Worse, if he feels neglected, he can become mesmerized into inactivity: then, he may merely trickle along. But he can usually recharge his battery and start over again.

WINTER WATER: Keyword – Enlivening

A winter baby who loves the swelling waters and extreme elements, you meet danger and enjoy a challenge. You unite strong feelings with deep contemplative powers; sometimes, those who know only one side of you may believe you are subdued and overshadowed by others. But you think wisely, feel things deeply, and rise to the occasion when you are required to do so. You feel a lot of responsibility even though you're not the eldest; winter makes you aware of the rhythm of life, its demands, and the need to grow tall sometimes. Though respected at work and thought steady by all, you can suddenly flash into clever conversation and show brilliance when it is needed. You stop people from getting out of control but, full of potential energy as you are, you can burst your own banks if pushed. Minimalist at home, you do things your way, and like to be well regarded. You are passionate about your interests and a good parent. But do let go of the past and forgive those who have not expressed themselves fully to you. You are a source of vitality when you are positive and happy in your skin.

SPRING WATER: Keyword – Invigorated

As a child, you probably seemed steady and self-contained compared with your vibrant siblings; but you are really happy finding things yourself, bubbling ceaselessly in your own company, needing no others to stimulate you. Born with an old head on young shoulders, you are emotionally and intellectually alive, seeing all, saying only what is called for you to say. You can stick at anything that interests you with a tenacity that others shouldn't neglect; this usually helps you to achieve your goals. More like a lively spring than a meandering river or unpredictable sea, you have lots of curiosity and keep on pushing gently away at things. You like the unconventional, love to explore and ponder someone's meanings and motives. A sense of humour prevents you from taking things too much to heart; and an eternal well of positive energy helps you along. You are astute and reasonable, but beware being indecisive at times, which will cost you dearly. You are also open to mood swings – largely depending on the company you keep!

SUMMER WATER: Keyword – Courageous

You are active, even when at leisure. With immense personal fortitude, you like brisk walks and sports, and excel in competition. You get on with the job, quietly and without any fuss, while others are still thinking about it. You are kind, helpful to your neighbours, and remember birthdays. Not necessarily romantic, you do like to catch people by surprise at times. You can change from tears to laughter in a moment, and need understanding friends who can guess your reasons. Quite enigmatic, you are a reminder that still waters run deep, and that no one who knows you knows the whole of you! Though apparently easy-going, you can dig your heels in, and life is never dull around you. Good at finance but also at taking risks, you make a good entrepreneur. But you can also be a complete couch potato, stuck in a chair, if no one stimulates or enthuses you. Losing your gentle competitive edge would be a misfortune, as it is this that brings out your courage and true grit.

AUTUMN WATER: Keyword – Inspiration

You are surprisingly melancholy and pensive at times, even though you are occasionally given to temper flare-ups! You are a negotiator, looking for ways to bring people together, or to bring about peace. Never having had all the attention on you, you have found amazing ways to mediate and wiggle in through a door of possibility. You probe into others' psyches, and can be both pensive and playful according to what you find. You can stir people up, triggering memories and emotions from the past. Not sexist or chauvinist, you tolerate people's idiosyncrasies, but you have exacting performance standards for yourself and for others, too. You are perhaps the most romantic water: like a sea in full moonlight, sparkling and scented to stir the imagination. But you may also have a secret life! When negative you are temperamental and suffer emotional high-water marks. Usually, however, you find the courage and inspiration to rise above it eventually.

MOUNTAIN

All third (and subsequent) sons

Mountains are the lookouts of the world. Standing tall, seeing far, being seen for miles, they have a visionary quality. They are a world unto themselves, a space where we sit, rest, consider and pause before we climb down. Mountain reaches from earth to the heavens: he aspires, and is focused. Tolerant and courageous, he is still, strong and dependable. He may be lofty and unapproachable, but still intriguing. While Thunder has something to say, and Water murmurs quietly, Mountain may be silent and hard to gauge. He will sit tight until approached, and may see everything, but say nothing. Yet he is a comfort: he is old and wise, sometimes tranquil and sometimes stormy, an enigmatic physical presence.

Mountain's potential Immensely strong, often proud and silent, you are honest and fairly balanced. You are charming, intelligent and exuberant, with a keen interest in life. You hold back until you know someone, so may be misread as shy or aloof. With your head in the clouds you are a dreamer, an ideas person – creative, contemplative, yet also grounded. You are considerate, pensive, and discreet. You like fresh ideas and unique opportunities. You have the ability to persuade people to do things they normally might not try. You may be absent minded, your head on higher things; and you are a complex character. You go where angels fear to tread, but you find yourself protected too!

Mountain's challenges Mostly, you are the strong, silent type, balanced with friendliness on the right occasion. But oh! When in a negative mood, you are quick to anger, prone to nervousness, and could have a breakdown if you allow the pressure to get to you. Like a volcano that builds up, you can suddenly blow; try to let off steam in a controlled environment. As a child, you may have created an imaginary world which has encouraged in you the habit of solitude and hypersensitivity. Don't allow your feelings to become blocked, and watch out for over-reaction, intellectual and emotional exhaustion,

WINTER MOUNTAIN: Keyword – Dignified

With an apparent haughtiness that comes from a nobility of spirit, some people wrongly feel you cannot do anything mundane; but you are a pillar of strength in almost all situations, able to get through a demanding routine as well as challenging changes. You instil confidence in others, making them feel secure, and often you become the family anchor. You can be a bit dogmatic in your opinions, and even obsessive; but you are learned, scholarly, patient, and a good teacher. You have suffered heartbreak, been troubled by the past, and perhaps become too analytical; but over time, this gives you persistence in what is important to you, and you will have gained confidence and stamina through experience. You are moral, upright, and your dignity has an empowering effect on other people. Appreciating what is sacred, you are grounded and loyal; but try not to become fixated on past disappointments or gloomy ideas. You would then be selling yourself short.

SPRING MOUNTAIN: Keyword – Sacredness

You may have little concern for authority – it is your intuition and inner religious feelings that govern your moral code. You love the past, the history of spiritual experience, and you may be interested in archaeology; but you also forge new thoughts, break from convention, and understand much about people and circumstances through meditation and inner vision. You are far from immature, and yet fresh experiences delight you. You may love simple pleasures, feel really affectionate to family and friends, and enjoy the special nature of each get together. You make time for other people, and enjoy working in the field of public relations. Yet you will be happiest, perhaps, working quietly by yourself, getting on with things in your own way, as you don't like being told what to do by anyone in command. You hate interference, and will be uneasy if you feel your soul or spiritual concepts are being attacked. Self-doubts are rare, but when they come, they eclipse your wisdom and enlightened mind. Find a good expression for your talents, as you may become listless if you can't find your true direction in life.

SUMMER MOUNTAIN: Keyword – Purposeful

You see more than other people even know exists. Opportunities, you understand, are everywhere, and you have the ambition and drive to utilize them. You have both wisdom and a measure of luck to help you through life and, being naturally spiritual and quite philosophical, you take most obstacles in your stride. You can be blunt at times, unaware that you are hurting anyone; this is partly because you wouldn't take offence yourself. Usually optimistic, your imagination and creativity are inspirational to others. Good at academic work, and sometimes sports, you are also sexy and humorous, enjoy taking risks, and love to flirt. Even when you're calm, something is probably smouldering away on the inside. You delve into secrets and mysteries, and have many interests. Burn-out can be a problem, as your mind is ceaselessly seething; and mental exhaustion may lead to other nervous disorders. However, your basic cheerfulness normally rescues you after a while.

AUTUMN MOUNTAIN: Keyword – Penetrating

You have an astonishing degree of self-acceptance. Aware of your faults and attuned to your talents, you are a quick thinker, an experienced reader of people, humorous, clever, but sometimes a little bit brash. Like Summer Mountains, you are alive to your opportunities, and you are good at motivating other people when they feel lost. You like a job that is totally involving, asking you to stretch and show your ability to blend new colours from new palettes. And, in fact, colour is important to you. You are vibrant yourself and will shun neutral colours most of the time. You are likely to be the man in a red shirt, or wearing yellow socks; 'dull' and 'safe' are not adjectives for your style. You have physical stamina, and might try flying planes or bungee-jumping; heights certainly don't worry you. You are loyal in relationships, but enjoy varied company. If you are overtired or undervalued you will oscillate between sadness and happiness, or you may forget things and become isolated. But you are mostly a sparkling catalyst who can easily get to the bottom of problems and find solutions quickly.

SKY

All fathers of all seasons

The Sky is our umbrella. It is moody and changeable, vast and unimaginable, often almost invisible, and yet forever there. In itself it is unfathomable, its being extends before and after us, its influence is unending, and its deepest feelings seem untouchable. It is our heaven, our security, and the backdrop to our tiny sense of ourselves. It is the home of angels, a haven for our dreams, and the dominion of flight and endless potential. It may also cloud over suddenly, become grey and threatening, and close in upon us. The Sky symbolizes the infinite, the parent of the chain of life and all imagined creation. It is the masculine divine, parent to all of us, bestowing a measure of divinity upon each one of us.

Sky's potential Sky, the Father, wishes for position, admiration, purpose, and just 'to be'. When functioning at the top of his wisdom, with a full and unchecked expression of his talents and strengths, when well educated and well loved, Sky is conscientious, non-judgemental, knowledgeable, and persuasive. He is realistic, balanced and honest. He seeks truth and purpose, with a strong sense of right and wrong, and is open to all ideas — though he is guided by logic. Spirituality is also an instinctive goal. At his best, Sky is tolerant and attracts respect. Man, once he has become a Father, gains wisdom, thinking beyond the self, and receives the respect and congratulations of his friends.

Sky's challenges When unable to seize his opportunities or articulate his views, Sky becomes critical, sarcastic and arrogant. Seeking perfection in a world that seems so far short of the mark, he becomes disconsolate about life. When he makes mistakes, he feels exasperated and cannot forgive himself, which in turn makes him self-righteous and dogmatic. Sky's challenge is to understand that his heart is in the right place, but that he should not sermonize. He needs to cultivate his humour and not give in to shame, as he makes the mistakes that are inevitably part of the human learning curve.

WINTER SKY: Keyword – Wisdom

Compassionate and interesting, just as enigmatic as all the Sky personalities, you have an air of mystery about you. Frequently clouding over with serious thought and tests of fortitude, you have a maturity and conscientiousness that encourages us all to endure the necessary times of introspection. You exude confidence – the capacity to wait with patience and watch the inevitable changes that will come. You are impetuous, but also secretive. You understand the quietest workings within the universe. You accept the reality of fears, but you deal with them. Your greatest challenge is to feel freely and express yourself emotionally: you allow blockages from the past to sit heavily with you. Learn to be wary of those feelings of disconnection from others. You know change is inevitable, but it is still and always worth making ties and putting down roots. Your most positive trait is your capacity for acceptance and your ability to look deeply within yourself and others. What you must challenge within yourself is a tendency to dwell on grief as a mode of self-expression, and too much repression of your feelings.

SPRING SKY: Keyword – Vitality

Enthusiastic, creative, optimistic and comforting, you are the soul of dawning light. You have energy and passionate interest in the world, yet you move with perfect calm into unknown places. When a storm is raging around you, you remain focused and balanced; the winds may howl, but you have seen it before, and you know that all will be well again. The Sky watches and waits, patiently, for tranquillity to return – as it always will. You don't gossip, and can keep the closest secrets. You may sometimes be restless, searching for new ideas and influences in fresh faces and places; but you always settle down again. A breath of fresh air is all it takes to find your centred self again. For others, you bring logic and emotional balance; for yourself, you may need to fight mood swings or a lack of cohesive thinking. If you are feeling stressed and out of sorts, you can sometimes become heated and irrational. However, your great strength is your ability to recover emotional clarity and balance, and your noblest nature is both sheltering and kind.

SUMMER SKY: Keyword – Meditative

Deep thinking and warm, you are the embodiment of the divine (male) spirit in full summer. The summer sky surprises us from time to time – catching us out, testing our preparations for life. It reflects our ideas back to us, like a wise judge, or a non-judgemental parent. You have moods and faces than we often misunderstand. On a sunny day, Summer Sky is an endless blue stretching to infinity, peaceful and full of insights. You are positive, with a sense of self-esteem – usually without arrogance or selfishness. You are open to others' ideas, sensual, and expressive; you know your direction in life. You are a wise old soul, whose instincts are good. Deep thought has given you an intuitive ability to support other people through crises. Your one difficulty can come from frustration; if you are denied full expression, you can become cynical, obsessive, and manipulative. But your strength is your exceptional sensitivity to life's nuances and, if you can avoid dwelling on the past, you offer those close to you someone to trust with whom they can find peace.

AUTUMN SKY: Keyword – Generosity

You have strength. wisdom and intelligence. Like the magical blend of late, warm days and skies, you have a huge range of experience and understanding, exceptional charisma, charm, and willpower. Your strong personal experience of the spiritual and the vast gives you an understanding of grief, loss, and pain. You see both sides of a story, knowing how to advise life's lost souls. Your capacity to change and embrace new directions is one of your greatest strengths – you can help friends and loved ones to cope with change, to see the best in it, to let go of the past and move forward. Earthly pleasures may not be so important to you – yet you love to share good times with friends. You may not covet things of beauty, but you appreciate them. You are generous with your time and support, helping uneasy souls to find themselves. . But your own challenge is not to become rigid, nor to give in to regrets or lack of concentration. Sometimes your passions run high and you become strangely fearful. But your patience, and pure heart, will usually rescue you.

How to find your fortune

This oracle contains 64 forecasts, each of which represents a symbolic picture of our state of mind in relationships with life and others, at that particular time. The forecast you attract enacts the appropriate circumstances for you at the time when you consult it.

To find the forecast that refers to your current situation

Decide on a question. It might be simple, demanding a basic 'yes' or a 'no' answer while offering scope for further information to illuminate the situation. Or it might be general, about the immediate direction of your future, or what will come up over the next year. Once you have formulated a question in your mind, take the three coins (or you can use three of the same value, size and weight, in which case head = sun, tail = moon). Throw the coins once and see whether you have suns or moons, and in which combination. Make a note of the result as follows:

3 suns – a moving sun line – put a cross through the sun symbol
3 moons – a moving moon line – put a cross through the moon symbol
2 suns/1 moon – a plain sun sign
2 moons/1 sun – a plain moon sign

Throw the coins six times in total, keeping your question in mind throughout. Each time you throw, record it as shown above with a sun or moon sign. Working from the bottom up, create a vertical tablet of six suns and/or moons. If you get a moving line, put a cross through the sun or moon symbol when you record it, as shown above. A plain line will be shown as an ordinary sun or moon.

By consulting the chart opposite, you will find the number of your forecast. Match the bottom three symbols of your tablet (your first three throws) to those in the vertical column. Match the top three symbols (your last three throws) to those in the horizontal column. Where these two lines meet on the chart is your forecast number.

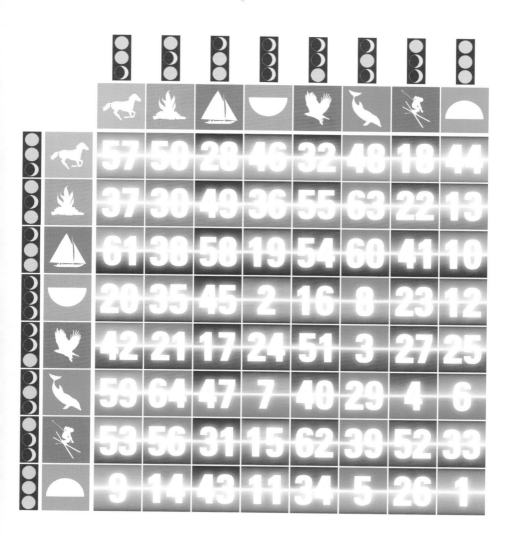

If you have thrown a moving sun or moon line this is regarded as being so rigid that it must eventually give way to the opposite; so a crossed sun would become a plain moon and vice versa. Note any moving line(s), then draw your tablet of symbols a second time, changing a crossed sun to a moon and a crossed moon to a sun. This makes a new tablet, giving you a second forecast number on the chart . You should read this forecast after the first one, as it will indicate how things will change shortly.

How to read your forecast

Turn to the page on which your numbered forecast appears. Your main forecast represents a detailed (but metaphoric) picture of your life, and the circumstances that surround you, right now at the present time. First, read the main commentary and consider how the forecast applies to your circumstances. Then, read the comments made about the individual moving lines that apply to you: for instance, if your second and fifth throws gave you three coins of a kind, and therefore a moving line, you should read what it says just for that specific line. Don't worry about all the other lines – just read those that apply to you. It may be that you have no moving lines, that none of your throws produced three of a kind, in which case you read just the main forecast.

If you do have any moving lines, now is the time to redraw your tablet, with suns replacing moons, or moons suns, where appropriate. You should read this extra forecast second; it will indicate where things are going to move to in your life in the near future and it gives you an idea of the outcome of the current circumstances. In this second reading, disregard the commentary on the individual moving lines; they apply only to your first reading.

How to use the forecast to your best advantage

While you consult your forecast or forecasts, consider what they mean in the light of your question. Every forecast offers advice as to how to come through any difficulties or challenges – of course, this is only advice, and if you do or don't follow it, the outcome will be up to you. The oracle always considers what a 'superior' man would do – this is someone who is wise and whom we might aspire to be. The 'inferior' man is likely to make mistakes. If you can follow the advice of the oracle, it offers you a way of ensuring the best possible outcome from your present situation. It also helps you to understand how any other people involved in your situation are thinking and feeling and, from this, you can learn how to work in tandem with them, to your best advantage.

Your Personality Profile and your forecast

When you first look at your forecast, check whether it includes one of the elements of your personality. The picture of the forecast will show you the symbols of the two elements that make it up – one in the top right corner and one in the bottom left corner. If, for example, you are a second daughter – Fire – and the Fire symbol is one of the two components shown on your forecast, then the reading itself has even greater personal relevance for you; it is made up of some of the metaphorical aspects of your own nature. Fifteen of the 64 forecast readings will have your Personality Profile within them: one, indeed, will be a double of your profile, with the same element above and below. Whenever your element appears in a reading, it means that the forecast is aimed even more specifically at you; this indicates that the time ahead for you is especially important, and the effects of the reading will be felt for some time.

To a lesser extent, but still important, you might take extra note of any reading that includes the element(s) of someone you are asking about. For instance, if your question concerns a relationship, and the person in your relationship is, say, Thunder, or Mountain, and you get a forecast that includes one of these elements, then it, too, has special and extra relevance. Try to understand the way in which the symbol itself is influencing the picture of the reading; it will offer you added insights about the way the other person is feeling. Pay special attention to these crucial moments, and make note of the answers you have got, keeping a record over time.

1 The rainbow

As this forecast is made up of two Sky trigrams it has special significance if you are a father, or if the question concerns your father.

Creative achievement and sublime success. You are the favourite child of Fortune now and will achieve just what you wish, thanks mainly to your untiring efforts and understanding of what it requires to succeed. Your creative thoughts are at their peak, your mind is attuned to others and yet properly also with the self; and your heart is full of optimism and certainty. You deserve acclaim. Actions and decisions you take now will alter your whole life for the better. You must persevere in what you know is the right thing to do: in this way you will be rewarded with true happiness. Your visions are true and your mental clarity is excellent. Time has a part to play – for you are choosing a goal that requires some time to come to full fruition. However, every step you take towards your wish makes each subsequent step even easier: the road improves and the going gets better as you move along. This forecast is connected with the late spring, when its power comes to full expression. This is a lucky moment also in the year ahead for you.

Much of what you will do requires creative imagination, and this you have. Organization is vital to your success, so you must put everything in order – not least, ordering what tasks must come before others. But the gods smile on you, and you have the courage and energy to perform well. You need strength, and you have it. You are developing wonderfully as an individual.

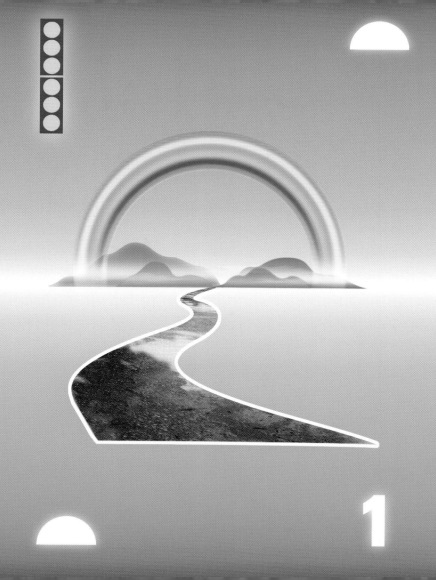

The moving lines

If any of your throws produced three identical coins (suns or moons), this is called a moving line. Read the relevant line(s) below, then change the line(s) to the opposite symbol, and look up and read the new forecast (see pages 44–5). Don't forget that your tablet of throws is written from the bottom up, so your first throw is the bottom one.

● If all your coins for the first throw were suns: This suggests that you are still in the planning stage. Your thoughts and ideas are good, but you need to make proper arrangements before setting out on your journey. Your worth may not yet have been recognized by others, but time is on your side. Plan a little more, and be patient.

● If all your coins in the second throw were suns: opportunities are starting to show themselves. It is the right time to declare your interests, and to take some steps towards securing your aims. Your reliability is beginning to be appreciated, and your influence can be felt in important areas.

● If all the coins in the third throw were suns: pressure begins to build up, and you have many things to attend to – both duties and creative obligations. There is not much time for rest, but the future is brightening and, if you are strong and dedicated now, the results you would hope for become easier to find. However, don't let too much ambition cloud your moral judgement.

- Three suns in the fourth throw: a crossroads has been reached. You have two strong potential paths before you, one of which suggests public success and acclaim, and the other, a more private feeling of achievement and happiness. Either choice is a good one and either may be the right one for you. There is no advice anyone else can offer, but know that the choice is for your heart alone.

- Three sun coins in the fifth throw: you are reaching the zenith of your powers, mentally and creatively, and a life in the full sunshine is unfolding. Fame and success seem certain; you have made a choice that requires confidence and will test your ability to stay true to yourself. Giddy heights arise, but you can keep your feet on the ground if you try.

- If your sixth and last throw is all sun coins: this suggests some humility is required. You are bright, energetic, creative and successful, but it is a test of your character not to give in to arrogant behaviour. If you can find modesty despite great personal success, you will maintain happiness and true friends.

- In the rare instance that all your lines were all suns, the forecast is especially powerful, and bestows added good fortune. Your future builds and shows that you have a true blend of masculine and feminine energy, strength and grace.

2 A lush harvest

As this forecast is made up of two Earth trigrams, it is especially potent for you if you are Earth, a mother; it is also extra important if your question concerned your own mother in any way.

Supreme success! This reading suggests that perfect success awaits you. What is required at this moment is an understanding that achievement comes through co-productions. Work with another talented soul, even if they receive more apparent praise than you do. However, equal success is yours. Your contributions are vital to many people. You are about to receive an award for being Best Supporting Actress: only an insecure person would see this as second best. Unlike the one in the limelight, you will achieve not only material success but also even greater spiritual success. Events unfolding now will see you achieve a principal goal in your life; but you also grow in wisdom and happiness. You are in balance, and understand yourself. You do not need loud applause from other people. You are nourished in every way: love, physical health, creative and material fulfilment. You may feel close to nature, and understand that the way forward depends on working in tandem with a powerful partner. Be guided by this person in confidence and you will achieve all that you could wish – unless your confidence is weak and your ego needs greater feeding. Friends are around you for a good reason, and you recognize this.

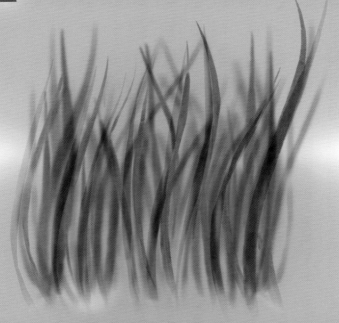

The moving lines

If any of your throws produced three identical coins (suns or moons), this is called a moving line. Read the relevant line(s) below, then change the line(s) to the opposite symbol, and look up and read the new forecast (see pages 44–5). Don't forget that your tablet of throws is written from the bottom up, so your first throw is the bottom one.

◗ If your first throw produced all moon coins: you must now make preparation for the future, being aware that a potentially difficult situation is ahead. Store money for the rainy days that are in the near future, or prepare more work than you were asked for. Providence comes if you are ahead of demand.

◗ When all the coins are moons in the second throw: you are guided by nature to do exactly what is right, and your inspiration comes from nature too. You need not search for a way to push yourself forward: the Earth is in harmony with you, and the best openings come of their own accord. Be quietly confident in what you are doing.

◗ Three moons in the third throw: act without vanity, and be prepared to work behind the scenes to achieve an excellent result for everyone. If you allow others to get all the attention, success will come, together with happiness and more personal freedom for you.

◗ All moons in the fourth throw: it would be wise for you to work quietly, and keep it to yourself, for the moment. Jealousy may arise if you attract too much attention, so be prepared to do much of the hard work without loud praise.

◗ All moons in the fifth throw: you will gain rewards if you are discreet. An outward appearance of modesty will benefit you more than being a self-publicist for now. The colour yellow will be fortunate for you.

◗ All moons in the sixth throw: be careful not to attract an enemy in a powerful position. There will be a time to push yourself forward, but that time is not now. Let others be in the firing line: it will be wisest for you to remain quiet and be focused yourself.

◗ In the rare instance that all the lines are complete moon lines, extra good fortune is implied. Personal modesty is natural to you and others will notice your worth of their own accord.

3 Sun emerges from clouds

Made up of Thunder and Water, this forecast is of extra significance if you are either the eldest son (Thunder) or the middle son (Water).

You will achieve success after perseverance. What you are striving for demands energy and there is difficulty in the early stages of the project. However, if you are brave and determined, you will surmount dangers and come out very well. Part of the problem now is that there is too much going on around you; you need to select what is really important and what is a diversion. What you want depends on being brave in some circumstances, for nothing is achieved without taking a risk and speaking up. If you want help, you must ask for it. It takes courage to put your thoughts and needs into words. However, if you don't ask for help, or if you stay put at home, you will not succeed. Therefore, this is the time to prepare your ideas, decide on a course of action and pursue it properly. Attacking your goal with determination will bring you through early difficulties and help you to find a clear way out of frustrations. A thunderstorm threatens: but this only clears the air. Perhaps you must undertake an interview for a job, or a reward, or a place on a course, and your nerves are under pressure. But if you can find the courage to prepare well and go through this test, you will be highly successful and grow as an individual. Be cheerful.

The moving lines

If any of your throws produced three identical coins (suns or moons), this is called a moving line. Read the relevant line(s) below, then change the line(s) to the opposite symbol, and look up and read the new forecast (see pages 44–5). Don't forget that your tablet of throws is written from the bottom up, so your first throw is the bottom one.

● If your first throw was all sun coins: your early actions have not been exactly right for success. You need to take a step backwards and think again of new ways to approach things. However, don't give up on your plans. It is simply necessary to rethink your strategy. Outright confrontation will not work well. Find a helper to work with or advise you.

◗ If your second throw is all moon coins: This is a special situation and you need to be very cautious. What you wish for is as yet out of reach; but loyalty to a cause will in fact be rewarded if you are able to wait. Don't be distracted by an offer of 'second best' from someone else; use your time to become as well qualified as possible.

◗ If all coins in the third throw are moons: there is no point pushing ahead now, because you are on unfamiliar ground. If you are wise you will decide on a new goal, and contain your angers and frustrations. This is not a time to venture into foreign pastures, but to look to the people and places you know well for good news and opportunities.

◗ All moons in the fourth throw: this is the time for taking the first step towards a resolution with another person. It is not a defeat if you have the strength to say that you need help, or are perhaps in the wrong. Brave actions will be rewarded: forgiveness, and new merits, will follow.

● If your fifth throw produces all suns: this is not the time to complain. Argument at present would be useless and would fall on deaf ears. Wait until a feeling of confidence returns to those around you; then, with effort and good humour, you will come through this critical moment.

◗ All moons in the final throw: testing conditions have caused a loss of confidence in you from the start. Perhaps you feel resigned to having to give in to another person's will; it would be wise to decide on a fresh course of action altogether and change your approach. Persistence now will be futile.

4 The mountain spring

This forecast is made up of Water and Mountain, so has particular application if you are either a second, or third, (or subsequent) son.

Success comes – eventually. There is a feeling here of success coming as someone without experience rushes in, literally, where angels fear to tread. Danger threatens but, unaware of the potential for difficulty, all is somehow well. In fact, this kind of naïve courage, that is associated with youth, is often a blessing. The way forward, at the moment, is to express enthusiasm and willingness, and even bravery, despite what common sense would seem to dictate. If you are prepared to get advice from someone who can channel your ideas and energy, and to charm a person in power, success will come. But it will not be immediate. You must be more modest than brash, and yet bold enough to ask for help from someone in a very revered position. It is also very important to listen and accept their advice the first time: do not ask for repetitions, or expect the answer to change. As with an oracle that you ask for guidance, ask in sincerity and take note of the answer. Do not annoy your advisor! Be prepared to work continuously towards a demanding goal, which will then grant you what you want. This forecast prophesies success for anyone who is bold enough to ask for help from a master at their craft; and who is strong enough to see through all that is required in order to get there.

4

The moving lines

If any of your throws produced three identical coins (suns or moons), this is called a moving line. Read the relevant line(s) below, then change the line(s) to the opposite symbol, and look up and read the new forecast (see pages 44–5). Don't forget that your tablet of throws is written from the bottom up, so your first throw is the bottom one.

◗ If your first throw gives you all moon coins: it is time to demonstrate self-discipline. You cannot put off a move towards greater maturity any longer. If you want to make progress and achieve something with your life, responsibility is now demanded, and you must be prepared to stick at it until the job is done. Some further education is implied.

● If the second throw produces all sun coins: you have not (yet) achieved full personal power, but you are wise and courteous in your relationships with other people and this will be lucky for you in the future. Someone around you is being silly, but you are not over-critical and you treat them with kindness. You may also need to take someone in need by the hand and help them out.

◗ If your third throw produces all moon coins: you are in danger of losing your own personality and sense of self by trying to act like another charismatic person. But this is not an answer. Don't lose sight of your own strength and character; and don't make yourself a doormat for anyone. Maintain your dignity.

○ If all the coins in your fourth throw are moons: be alert to the possibility that your wishes are only fantasies at present. It is important to fix on a really worthy course of action and not to set your sights – or your heart – where you cannot find happiness.

○ If all your coins in the fifth throw are moons: you have a child-like purity of heart, and you will charm those who can help you. Acting without arrogance, but with good faith and instinct, you are rightly ready to listen to someone who can help you progress; success and good fortune flow from this.

● All sun coins in the last throw: punishment looms, and it is important to keep it in proportion. Whether you are the one who must correct another's mistakes, or it is you who will be addressed, anger will not help matters at all. Be calm and fair.

5 Marking time

This forecast is made up of Sky and Water, so it is especially significant if you are either Sky (a father) or Water (the second son).

Success is assured after a short waiting period. Sometimes things cannot be hurried; pushing to try to speed up others' actions will only aggravate an existing relationship. The lesson for the moment is one of finding patience. What you want and need will certainly come, but only when it is ready. If this means that you must make temporary arrangements to deal with immediate needs, then so it must be. Energies spent in other fruitful activities will lessen the tension and fill up the waiting time. Keep busy. You need to feel sure of yourself, and to be truthful with others. It would be sensible to use this interval with cheerful energy and sense. Efforts spent fighting your circumstances will only make matters worse. Look after your own physical and psychological needs in any way that you can, and stay optimistic. The future is looking very good, but it is still the future.

Travel is also indicated in this reading. Perhaps travel will ease the present period of waiting; or it might also be that travel would improve immediate conditions and ignite additional opportunities. A trip across water (or overseas) is very likely.

5

The moving lines

If any of your throws produced three identical coins (suns or moons), this is called a moving line. Read the relevant line(s) below, then change the line(s) to the opposite symbol, and look up and read the new forecast (see pages 44–5). Don't forget that your tablet of throws is written from the bottom up, so your first throw is the bottom one.

● If your first throw (the bottom line) is all sun coins: you have a feeling that difficulties might be ahead, even though they have not yet become obvious. Problems might arise, but it won't help to watch out for them and waste time now. Keep focused on what you can and must do, and be positive that all will turn out if you remain sincere.

● If your second throw resulted in all sun coins: you must wait. Don't approach a tricky situation any sooner than you have to. Be careful not to get side-tracked by disagreements with others; and don't blame other people for your own predicament. A level head will find a way to move forward.

● If all coins in the third throw are suns: this is a very important moment in your life, requiring careful thought and diplomatic behaviour. You have misjudged a task and fallen short of the distance you had to travel; but it's best not to make any fresh mistakes now, or allow your behaviour to attract hostility. Act with caution, and recognize the serious time approaching.

○ All the coins in the fourth line are moons: you have walked into a situation that now requires a very calm head. Prior actions have brought this about and you have put yourself in an unenviable place. Fate must now play its hand, and the best way of weathering the storm is to act with courage and decorum. Only in this way might an escape from danger be found.

● If your fifth throw brings all sun coins: this line offers consolation. Be ready to preserve your strength, however and whenever you may; inner composure will help to bring you through what has been a transforming and testing episode. Good humour and a touch of self-mockery will win you friends and give you the energy to endure. Persevere with your actions, and all may yet come out well.

○ If your sixth and final throw produced all moons: this is the moment of truth, when you must face the consequences of previous actions. Do not try to run away. And strangely, at this critical moment, someone unexpected appears to take a hand in the outcome of all events. Be prepared that it may be better than you had hoped, or not as you had hoped: and yet, if you are sweet-natured, a happy conclusion will be the result.

6 A shower of rain

This forecast if made up of Water and Sky, so it is especially important if you are either the second son (Water), and/or the Sky, a father. You are facing a key moment in your life.

Fortune comes from finding a new strategy. You feel that you are in the right, but you are facing resistance from someone else. You are not forced to weather a savage storm, however, for it is only a shower. At the same time, it is unwise to ignore the rain and allow it to soak you without giving it due attention. Stop for a moment and collect your thoughts: run back for an umbrella. You need to find new ideas to meet the challenge of the day, and be properly prepared with exactly what you need in order to succeed. Most importantly, your head must be quite clear. You need to meet opposition from another quarter without anger, but well informed and with clarity of expression. Explain your points without enmity – and be ready to have to do so. A third party, who is quite impartial, can arbitrate and make a fair decision. This may mean a delay in the speed of your plans; but this temporary halt will eventually be to your advantage. Do not lose heart or temper, but remain very clear. If you are unsure of yourself at this moment you will run into difficulty. But under no circumstances should you underestimate the present weather. It is vital to give your proper attention to the right way to begin your venture.

The moving lines

If any of your throws produced three identical coins (suns or moons), this is called a moving line. Read the relevant line(s) below, then change the line(s) to the opposite symbol, and look up and read the new forecast (see pages 44–5). Don't forget that your tablet of throws is written from the bottom up, so your first throw is the bottom one.

◗ If you have thrown all moon coins in your first throw, it would be better not to attempt a contest with someone strong at the moment. Wait to see how heavy the rain will be, and take advantage of the moment to revise your plans a little. Try to avoid any open dispute.

● If your second throw produced all sun coins: it is better not to go into competition with another person at the moment. Their strength is superior to yours: they are better prepared at present. Draw back from a fight, and no disgrace will come from it. Your action may also be wiser for someone close to you.

◗ If all the coins were moons in the third throw: this is not the time to overspend! If you have been generous to others, or indulged in too many luxuries recently, it is time to be sensible and live on a budget. You will enjoy most what you honestly earn. Be especially cautious if you are trying to keep up with others who have more cash and a more extravagant lifestyle than yours.

● If the fourth throw produces all sun coins: this is a good moment to alter your way of looking at things and adjust your reactions. As if you have run back indoors from the rain, you have a chance to reconsider what will be in your best interest. In any case, arguments are best left without fuel. While the rain falls, think better of your intentions. Really good fortune ensues, if you can avoid a fight!

● If all the coins in your fifth throw are suns: Someone with sense and authority is now able to sort our your difficulties. It may be a person trained in law, or in accounting. Be ready to accept the excellent advice you are given, and good fortune will be assured.

● When the sixth and last throw produces all sun coins: someone may have appeared to win at a game, but this victory is hollow and will not last. Be patient, and be determined to revise your own ideas and look for peaceable ends to your problems.

7 The battle

This forecast, being made up of Water and Earth, has special importance if you are either the second son (Water), or Earth, a mother.

Good fortune comes from good organization. Here is a balance between danger and discipline. The image behind this forecast is of an army, great and strong, but held in check by a wise and disciplined general who uses all power to avoid a war, and who leads his soldiers without bullying them. Therefore, good fortune will come if you can influence those people around you who need to be organized, but do so without threat or force. It is important to achieve a cohesive effort through enthusiasm, and to harness the interests of those you need to work with for a happy and productive relationship. Just as a child will work at chores or tasks more cheerfully, and with better results, if their interest is engaged, so will those close to you whose help you need. Organization and self-discipline is crucial for success, and this sense of order must be communicated to others involved with you. Don't try to win points by being aggressive or dangerous; it is sometimes possible to demonstrate that you have powerful muscles *without* flexing them. Generous behaviour to others will result in your gaining more support and help. It may be necessary to train yourself to be physically fit and strong, to contribute to your mental agility and clarity. Self-discipline starts with physical discipline and a clear code of ethics.

The moving lines

If any of your throws produced three identical coins (suns or moons), this is called a moving line. Read the relevant line(s) below, then change the line(s) to the opposite symbol, and look up and read the new forecast (see pages 44–5). Don't forget that your tablet of throws is written from the bottom up, so your first throw is the bottom one.

In this forecast the lines, individually, are perhaps the most important part of the story:

◗ If your first throw brought all moon coins: order is very important in what you are trying to accomplish now. A duty must be allotted to each individual and carried out with precision. Make sure that what you want to embark on is fair and valid towards other people.

● If your second throw produces all sun coins: don't expect others to perform tasks or take on responsibilities you would not do yourself. If the times ahead are demanding – if there is much work, or a physically rigorous programme – be prepared to share in the hard work. If you are willing to get your own hands dirty, you will have real luck and make a great success of what you do.

◗ If your third throw produces three moon coins: too many cooks will spoil the broth. Someone must assume clear leadership and be prepared to make decisions. If other opinions are sought, it will be impossible to reconcile many different attitudes. Elect a leader to follow, and do so ungrudgingly.

◯ If your fourth throw is three moon coins: it might be better to retreat than to take on an opponent who is bigger or has more strength than you do. This is not always true, for sometimes one ought to stand up to a bully; but in this instance, finding a way to draw back would be better than being broken by authority.

◯ If your fifth throw results in all moon coins: to defeat someone who is unfairly taking advantage of you or making unwarranted demands, you must have support in numbers. Assemble a complaint which can be proven with many voices, and you will not be defeated.

◯ A sixth and final throw with all moon coins: you are on the verge of a great success. However, it is impossible to reward all the people you would wish to, so it is important to select only those who can truly handle the tasks that you would give them. Reward other people with praise, or thanks, or gifts; but not with power.

8 Holding hands

This forecast is made up of Earth and Water, so it is especially important for you if you are either Earth, a mother, or Water, the second son. For you, this represents a key moment in your life.

Good fortune comes from good partnership. This reading foretells happiness, success and good fortune, as a result of finding an accord with a few people close to you who are completely on your wavelength. The image of holding hands relates to the way that the earth holds water; when just the right balance is achieved, it is of mutual benefit: the grass being nourished by the water, the water finding a welcome in the rich earth. So, when you feel you have found a true partner or partners, you will attract good fortune by sticking together. You have a joint goal and a common wish to travel in the same direction. It will be important for you to consider whether, together, you have the character to endure some tests and deal with problems as they arise. Crises happen to everyone, but how you handle them is important. If you have enough trust in each other, then together you will defeat the issues that threaten your peace. Other people will gather around your banner now, and be led by you. This is a responsibility; but with honesty, you will find a way to utilize each individual's greatest talents, and achieve a runaway success. Thus, this reading is equally applicable in love or in career issues. In a love relationship, the focus is on two suited people, with different talents, holding hands tightly and winning through to happiness. In business, there may be a suggestion that more than two people are involved, and that many people with different strengths come together for a polished result. It suggests a group who all hold hands together and rise to the top, despite some stressful tests. This is a reading of wonderful fortune. It is also associated with springtime.

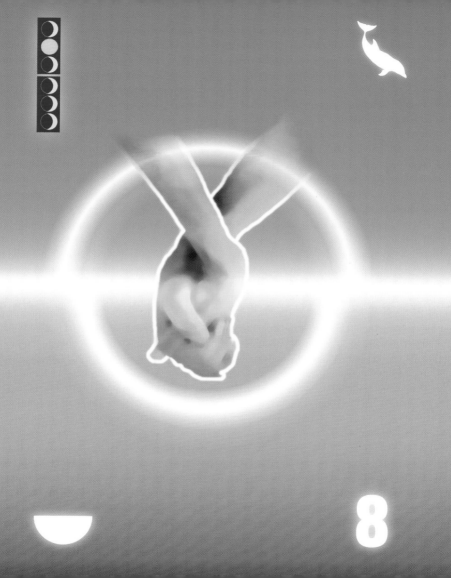

The moving lines

If any of your throws produced three identical coins (suns or moons), this is called a moving line. Read the relevant line(s) below, then change the line(s) to the opposite symbol, and look up and read the new forecast (see pages 44–5). Don't forget that your tablet of throws is written from the bottom up, so your first throw is the bottom one.

◗ If your first throw brought all moon coins: it is not charm or appearances that bring you close to another person, but honesty and integrity between you. Fortune is showered upon you from the world around you, as you attract such good feeling to you from those you meet and deal with.

◗ If your second throw was all moons: no matter how your loyalty is tested, you will hold fast to a key relationship, which will prove the right thing to do. Happiness will flow from your loyalty.

◗ If your third throw was all moons: people with whom you are intimate are not your equals: trying to reconcile greatly different values between you may lead to unhappy times ahead. Be pleasant to those with whom you must have social relationships, but avoid being drawn into closer partnership together than you know is wise.

◗ If your fourth throw produced all moon coins: you have a good relationship, probably of love, with someone you have known for some time, and it may be the right moment to be open about this with others. Don't be afraid that news of this tie will cause problems: good fortune comes from your honesty and determination.

● If your fifth throw produced all sun coins: there is no need to use tricks to gain a following or win your point; you will find that others come to you and follow your lead from their own independent choice. Your wisdom with people is tested, but trust in others' free judgement will pay off, and all will go well.

◗ If your last throw produced all moon coins: it is now urgent to decide whether to join with others in a project or plan, or let it go. If you miss this opportune moment to link up with others, the chance will be lost. Make a decision now, but don't regret your move later.

9 A child with power

This forecast is made up of Sky and Wind, so has extra significance if you are either Wind, the eldest sister, or Sky, a father. This is a significant moment in your life.

Success will come with gentle, consistent effort. Someone who is relatively without power, but who has intelligence, charm and humour, now has the ability to prevent someone with power from abusing their position. Outright confrontation is not the way to do this, but just as a laughing and well-loved child can wheedle a grumpy parent into following their wishes, so too can a wise person of lesser real power hold a tyrannical leader in check. It may be that the time has arrived for you to work hard to prevent an older person, who is in a higher position, from making unwise and selfish decisions which affect all around them adversely. Or it may be that you must attempt to change the decisions of a parent, or partner, who is in a position to make choices based on economic strengths. The way to do this is with gentle persuasiveness and lightness of touch. Success in all your ventures is possible, but you must find a way around the obstacles in your path. The key is to understand that this can be achieved better without open challenges, but by careful and sweet-tempered moves. This is the moment when those in a lower position, who behave in a gentle and intelligent way, will have power over the bigger fish. Influence over others, who may hold our futures in their hands, can be achieved only by being subtle. Later, change will come in a more sweeping way, but not yet. For the moment, take small steps with gentle humour, and you will achieve some measure of restraint over superiors.

The moving lines

If any of your throws produced three identical coins (suns or moons), this is called a moving line. Read the relevant line(s) below, then change the line(s) to the opposite symbol, and look up and read the new forecast (see pages 44–5). Don't forget that your tablet of throws is written from the bottom up, so your first throw is the bottom one.

● If your first throw produced all sun coins: it is understandable that you now wish to move forwards and press your affairs. But you may not make much headway at this time and, if you are forced to go back a step or two, or mark time a little longer, no harm or lasting loss will come from this.

● If your second throw produced all sun coins: your normal path is temporarily blocked and it may be advisable to stop and rethink matters, with a view to finding an alternative path altogether in the future. Don't set out for a picnic on a rainy day! Wait for the right and propitious moment to set out after your goals. Waiting for the ripe moment brings very good fortune.

● If your third throw produced three sun coins: the climate is still not right to push too far with your goals or wishes; it would be better to stay quiet. Even if things look positive for you to push for your point, you may underestimate the obstinacy of your opponents. Take your time.

○ All moon coins in the fourth throw: it will be difficult to hold a strong-willed person with power in place now, yet by expressing unselfish truths you will carry your point. Do so gently.

● When your fifth throw is all sun coins: your own feelings and good behaviour attracts support from others and you don't find yourself standing alone. As you use your humour to cope with a difficult individual, you win admirers and friends who will remain loyal to you. Good fortune is assured.

● A final throw with all sun coins: your perseverance and good temper, maintained under a critical gaze, bring final fruition. All of your subtle actions have now reached a climax of influence and a change for the better is on its way. A new regime will soon sweep through, and everyone will be relieved. But it is still important to act with political tact.

10 Act like a child

This forecast is made up of Lake and Sky, so has special significance for you if you are Lake, the third or youngest daughter, or Sky, the father.

Success comes from a humorous, childlike strategy. A young, energetic and cheerful person dares to make humorous demands of the person in authority, and comes to no harm. In fact, success comes from the good-natured exchange. Sometimes, it is safe for someone in a position of relative weakness to speak out against another person who is much stronger than they are, as long as it is done with cheerful spirits and warmth, rather than anger. Just as a child can ride upon the shoulders of an adult, laughing and making swift strides, so it is possible now to find an authority figure who will help you to make progress. Other people will be amazed to see you take on someone with a reputation for order and authority, but you will actually achieve significant progress, and make many important points, through your cheerful manner and playfulness. There is a difficult situation looming, and it may take the trusting goodness of a child to handle the situation. Sweet manners will succeed even with very grouchy people! So, adopt a child-like faith and refreshing honesty. Whether in business or in love, boldness born of real sweetness completely disarms the one in charge who, completely secure in his own position, finds it is easy to be benevolent and grants a wish. This is a moment of exceptional good fortune.

10

The moving lines

If any of your throws produced three identical coins (suns or moons), this is called a moving line. Read the relevant line(s) below, then change the line(s) to the opposite symbol, and look up and read the new forecast (see pages 44–5). Don't forget that your tablet of throws is written from the bottom up, so your first throw is the bottom one.

● If your first throw produces all sun coins: you have conducted yourself simply and without guile, and you are starting to make progress where it might least have been suspected by others. But you are lit by an inner cheerfulness, which guarantees that you win friends in high places. You are given a helping hand by a person in power.

● If your second throw produces all sun coins: you are content with your own ideas and thoughts, and know you are on the right path. Making progress is not your goal, but thinking deeply about life is more important. A dark man helps you, and you will attract good fortune.

◗ Your third throw brings three moon coins: do not yet undertake any tasks that are beyond your strength. Like a person seeing with only one good eye, you cannot judge the whole situation. Don't put yourself in the firing line, or take on dangerous missions. This is not the moment for recklessness.

- If your fourth throw brings all sun coins: this time, you face a situation fraught with inherent danger, but you are now in a position to succeed because you are lit with inner strength and are fully prepared. In fact, you will survive a dangerous position by being ready to move forwards. Again, a person in power gives you a lift up!

- If the fifth throw produces all sun coins: conscious of difficulties, you find a way to get out of them. Success comes at a crucial time and by getting help from higher places, but this is achieved only because you are aware of the possible problems and have seen the whole picture.

- Your sixth and final throw produces all sun coins: you have cheerfully worked through many demanding tasks, staying positive and focused under duress. Now, the hard work is at an end and if, the job has been done well, as it seems, a really excellent result comes to you. You are riding laughing on the shoulders of a great man. Luck is with you, partly since you have worked wisely and well.

11 Tranquillity

This reading is made up of Sky and Earth, so is most significant if you are a father (Sky) or a mother (Earth), or if your question concerns either of your parents.

Peace and harmony settles around you – supreme success. This reading has an affinity with that time in early spring, at the equinox, when heaven is at one with the earth on which we live. All is in balance: night and day are of equal length. When earth and sky are united as one, there is peace. All arguments are over, all tensions dissolved, and all those who are important to you are getting on well with each other. At this moment, people in authority show goodwill and cheerfulness to those who depend on them. Equally, those who must work in junior positions are happy to do so. There is a feeling of harmony and of everything working well and efficiently. People who are truly good, and wise, and kindly towards others, are in positions of power – and they can be trusted. Equally, those who approach life and their fellows with the right attitude will succeed, while those who are unpleasant, ungenerous, or uncaring of others, will lose influence. The higher instincts are balanced in our minds, and rule our behaviour: guided by the best motives, we achieve the best results for everyone close to us. Those who are small-minded or bad-tempered are defeated – it is even possible that someone who is genuinely wicked will be removed from power. This is a true time of prosperity. If you have questions to ask, or favours to beg, from those who are in power, this is the perfect time. Goodwill comes from those above you. And if you need help from someone of authority, even in a personal matter, this would be a good time to ask for it. Besides this, there is a feeling of springtime around you now – whatever the season! Take this literally: give your attention to the garden, and to other projects in their infancy. Everything looks fertile and positive. The gods come to earth to lend a hand!

11

The moving lines

If any of your throws produced three identical coins (suns or moons), this is called a moving line. Read the relevant line(s) below, then change the line(s) to the opposite symbol, and look up and read the new forecast (see pages 44–5). Don't forget that your tablet of throws is written from the bottom up, so your first throw is the bottom one.

● If your first throw produced all sun coins: just as fresh grass when it is pulled up brings soil with it, you have at present the power to get other people on board when you start a project. Many will follow your lead, and this is a good time to exert your influence. Success follows you.

● If your second throw brought all sun coins: you have many diverse ideas in perfect balance. You are aware of the need to be kind and patient with those around you who have less ability than you do; and you also understand that with each action you take, parts of your plan that are at present in the distance will come into focus in time. You have an eye on both the present and the future, and much tolerance for others. Good fortune comes.

● If your third throw produced all sun coins: you are aware of the need to stockpile today against possible lack tomorrow. There is such a flowing of bounty now, that you would be wise to save something for a rainy day. Fortune goes in cycles: this is a time to make plans and budget for tomorrow. In this way, good fortune will stay with you, as a result of your common sense.

◗ If your fourth throw produced three moon coins: you are sensitive to those who are less successful in terms of money and power, and you are careful not to boast of your achievements or show off your possessions to make them feel worse. Good fortune comes to you for such sensitivity.

◗ The fifth throw brought three moon coins: the princess marries a commoner – this shows the union of higher- and lower-placed people making harmony together. Modesty comes from those in high places; many blessings flow from such wisdom and good nature. Supreme success comes to you now.

◗ The final throw produced all moon coins: a change of fate is likely, and it is best to accept a setback now if it comes. This will have no lasting impact, but may tie your hands for the moment. Attempts to fight it would only bring greater difficulties, or lasting enmity. It is better to be ready to withdraw, and wait for a new day.

12 Decay

Composed of Earth and Sky, this forecast signifies an important moment if you are either a mother (Earth) or a father (Sky).

This reading suggests a time of waiting. It is the inverse of the previous one, where Earth is above the Sky, suggesting balance. Here, the Sky is moving away from us here on Earth, and relationships between those in power and those in the lower echelons are not in such balance. Unfortunately, this is the moment when those who are bad-tempered, or morally questionable, or even jealous of your abilities, may gain precedence. Those of weaker intellect seem to be given positions of power. You will see the world around you as unfair, perhaps. But don't despair: simply, see this as the position in this moment. The present circumstances will test your personal courage and sense of inner worth. If you can examine these and still believe in your own talents and abilities, and recognize what is the right way to behave, you will come out well in the end. Don't be drawn into false values by others: don't let people of inferior mind or personality lead you into activities with which you are not comfortable. Stay true to yourself, and wait to voice your true feelings on another day, in a different climate. In this way you maintain your own worth, and secure your future. Depend on your own inner resources, and stay silent if necessary. Ultimately, after a period of chaos and decay, the pendulum will swing back again, and order will be restored.

12

The moving lines

If any of your throws produced three identical coins (suns or moons), this is called a moving line. Read the relevant line(s) below, then change the line(s) to the opposite symbol, and look up and read the new forecast (see pages 44–5). Don't forget that your tablet of throws is written from the bottom up, so your first throw is the bottom one.

○ If your first throw gives all moon coins: it may not be possible at present to have your feelings heard, or make an impact on others. Be ready to resist the pleas of someone who wants you to join in a silly plan. Stand firm!

○ If your second throw results in all moon coins: be willing to suffer for having a different point of view. Those without wisdom and innate goodness will flatter superiors to gain promotion. But be sure not to pay lip service yourself to the deeds of others when you know them to be wrong.

○ If the third throw brings all moon coins: a turning point is ahead. Some people have risen up the ladder under false pretensions. They don't have the ability, or the talent, to justify their promotion. But don't complain – just let fate take its course.

● When the fourth throw produces all sun coins: there has been a standstill, a waiting period while chaos was everywhere. Now, this is coming to an end. For the person who has refused to join in the anarchy, or be false to his or her true ideals, a release comes from the madness. Progress can soon be made again.

● If the fifth throw results in all sun coins: the gossip who held the ear of the person in charge has lost influence, and there is now an investigation into the right way to do things. The cheat can no longer hide; your personal problems are nearly at an end.

● The sixth and last throw produces all sun coins: in a state of emergency normal life is put to one side. But now, the emergency is coming to its end, and very shortly normal happy life will be able to resume. A good leader helps to re-establish calm and order; and for those who have kept their heads – and their good manners – all will now be well. Good fortune comes at last.

13 A beautiful sunset

This reading is made up of Fire and Sky, so is especially important for you if you are either a second daughter (Fire), or a father (Sky). This marks a defining moment for you.

This is a very positive reading. Real success is accomplished through powerful friendship and two or more people coming together with a united aim and a fascinating cause. There are times when it is difficult to tackle a demanding project; but if you have a good team working alongside you – and particularly, a feeling of good fellowship between you – you can accomplish the most demanding feats. This is a moment for togetherness: the image of a glowing sunset suggests a good day's work accomplished and friends enjoying the late beauty of the day. But there is still a lot of work ahead. What will succeed for you now is that your wishes should be important not only to you, but to at least one other person who is helping you. You are not being selfish in your aims; there is good sense, and a feeling that several people will benefit, if you succeed at your task. In some way, your goals now are good for humanity as a whole. And, there is a unity in your thinking with other people. You are part way along a long and challenging path: this may be personal, concerning study or even love, or it may concern your career aspirations. But you still have some way to go, and there may still be very difficult days ahead of you. Yet, with optimistic thinking and a good relationship between you and those involved with you, you will make lighter of the drudgery, or even the dangers, that might have prevented lesser spirits from trying to succeed. Organization is of the utmost importance, and someone must lead from the front. Whether you are the leader, or agree to be ably led by a bright and dynamic person, success seems assured. A strong feeling of friendship makes the journey much less worrying. And a journey in the physical sense is also definitely ahead. Get ready to pack your bags and travel with at least one other person.

13

The moving lines

If any of your throws produced three identical coins (suns or moons), this is called a moving line. Read the relevant line(s) below, then change the line(s) to the opposite symbol, and look up and read the new forecast (see pages 44–5). Don't forget that your tablet of throws is written from the bottom up, so your first throw is the bottom one.

● If the first throw produces all sun coins: everything is out in the open. Friendship and your ventures succeed because there is no secrecy or going behind the back of anyone. Many friends join together for an adventure, and they are genuinely attached to each other. Good fortune is with you!

◗ If your second throw gives three moon coins: there may possibly be a difference of opinion between members of a group. Some have their own interests, which are not in the same direction as the main adventure. Be careful not to be caught up in politics among friends.

● If your third throw results in all sun coins: there is some mistrust between friends now, and this could be destructive. It is important not to let anyone sow seeds of doubt with regard to a close relationship. Do not be led into suspicions that are beneath you. If you are led away from good fellow feeling, your present aims will falter. Stay true to yourself and your friends.

● If your fourth throw gives all sun coins: you are coming to the resolution of a quarrel. You may see things differently from someone very important to you; but by refusing to fight, and by standing at a distance from the affair, you achieve a happy and positive result. Good fortune comes with this line.

● If your fifth throw is all suns: you may feel very closely connected with a special individual, but circumstances contrive to keep you apart – perhaps even physically. But happily, if your hearts are close, circumstances will eventually be overcome, even if you must pursue a somewhat circuitous path to happiness. Be brave! Success comes if you are truly patient. The image is of reunion after a forced break in a love affair.

● If your last throw is all suns: you are in a position where you must work with someone or several people who you do not warm to; however, any efforts you make at friendly civility, if not real closeness, will be ultimately rewarding. You have good intentions, and they ensure your success.

14 Rise to the top

This reading, made up of Sky and Fire, has special significance if you are a father (Sky) or the second daughter (Fire). In either instance this becomes a very important reading, suggesting a powerful moment in your life.

As a result of sense and quiet wisdom, everything comes good. This forecast describes success coming to a kind and gentle soul – someone who has been modest and played down their own self-importance. The image is of fire in the heavens, a glorious sunset and the end to a perfect day. More importantly, this is the perfect atmosphere into which to ascend; a time to float upwards and be showered with joy. This reading suggests that you have shown personal strength and good feeling, have thought clearly about what is important to you, what goals you strive for. You have recognized what is worth getting upset about and, more importantly, what is not! You have not been side-tracked, and you may have refused to become upset by thoughtless friends or loved ones. This is the kind of wisdom one might only hope to attain after a whole lifetime. All the signs are good for you at this time: the season, or the precise time and day, is exactly right for making the decision you have on your mind, or for setting out after a really important personal goal. Everything is in your favour: sunset illuminates the end of a beautiful day, and you can enjoy a moment of reflection after good work and good deeds for others. Your kindness and good sense pays dividends on a personal and material note, and career success and financial prosperity are truly in line now.

The moving lines

If any of your throws produced three identical coins (suns or moons), this is called a moving line. Read the relevant line(s) below, then change the line(s) to the opposite symbol, and look up and read the new forecast (see pages 44–5). Don't forget that your tablet of throws is written from the bottom up, so your first throw is the bottom one.

● If your first throw brings three sun coins: there is still a need for caution and steadiness. It is important to be aware that there are still some difficulties to overcome, and some aspects of your present aims need a pragmatic approach. This is a time to be unselfish, and refuse to rise to the provocations of others. Don't lose focus.

● If your second throw was three sun coins: there are several people who are prepared to help you – either to discuss and sound out ideas, or to be of actual practical help. If your house needs painting, get friends to pick up a brush! You are surrounded by those who wish you well and who will be there for you when they are needed. So, this is an excellent moment to go after something you want!

● If your third throw is all suns: this is a moment to share what you have with others; in particular, it may be the right time to offer help to someone in power, or who has a high position or influence. It is also the moment to be unselfish about what you have achieved, and your generosity will have powerful reverberations.

● If your fourth throw is all suns: don't be worried if you are associating with people who have greater wealth, or apparent affluence, than you. By being true to yourself, and refusing to be impressed or even dwarfed by them, success comes to you. You are behaving wisely, which is seen and noted.

◗ If the fifth throw produces all moon coins – you demonstrate real sincerity and purpose by your actions. You will win over many people, who see you as honest and fair. You have gone about your business – either personal or concerning work – with humour and good sense. You are accessible to other people: good fortune truly comes to you, and possessions are not important to you.

● Your sixth and final throw is all sun coins: the heavens rain blessings upon you! Wisdom and profound inner confidence have led you to praise the contributions of others and make little of your own, and the gods are delighted! As a result of your undemanding lack of fuss, you will win true admirers, true friends, and gain blessings from providence. You are not concerned with superficialities. Good fortune!

15 Modesty prevails

This forecast is composed of Mountain and Earth, so if you are either the third or youngest son (Mountain) or a mother (Earth), this reading has more significance for you and indicates a really important moment in your life.

Here, it is pure modesty that triumphs. This reading concerns quiet and unassuming behaviour. A series of actions and tasks undertaken result in outstanding success, largely because it is not the aim of the individual to be seen to win honours or achieve status. If this is your reading, you are not driven by a need to be recognized for what you do, or to be applauded for your actions. You see the merit of a quieter life, with achievements that are more personal to you. Some who achieve the pinnacle of fame may quite suddenly be forgotten – the sun at noon is at its peak, but will gradually decline towards sunset: what comes up, must go down. And the opposite is also true: in a cycle of growth, that which is small will become big again. Your behaviour is appreciated by neighbours, friends and peers, and also by the gods, for its apparent lack of concern with gaining awards or honours. Most importantly, you have gained respect from those whose good opinion is important to you. You see that the prize of fame and riches, sought by many, has but shallow appeal. Your good sense and concern with more important matters, which might well be unseen or unsung, ensure the fullest and richest life for you in what really counts. You are destined for greatness; but your wisdom and modesty are appreciated by everyone with sense. You will achieve so much, yet never boast of your achievements.

15

The moving lines

If any of your throws produced three identical coins (suns or moons), this is called a moving line. Read the relevant line(s) below, then change the line(s) to the opposite symbol, and look up and read the new forecast (see pages 44–5). Don't forget that your tablet of throws is written from the bottom up, so your first throw is the bottom one.

◗ If your first throw produces three moon coins: you have an important job to undertake, requiring simple, direct action, without fuss or demanding attention. The task may not be easy – but success will come if you set about it without making too much of what is ahead. It is modest, quiet action that produces results.

◗ If your second throw produces all moon coins: without looking for prizes or recognition, you set out to finish the work in front of you. You are not looking for praise, but in fact your actions speak louder than any words, and you gain good fortune.

● If your third throw brings all sun coins: because you are not trying to make a fuss about your work and your aims, but simply desire to get on with the things demanding your work and attention, you receive the greatest appreciation and praise, and true success. You are well placed to realize a dream; but in spite of the merits you receive, you stay modest and focused, feet on the ground.

◗ Your fourth throw produces all moon coins: you are not swayed by the attentions of people who call you great. You see things calmly, and still behave with dignity and modesty. At the same time, you verbally recognize the contributions of others. Success comes to you for your well-grounded behaviour.

◗ The fifth throw produces all moon coins: modest behaviour should not be confused with letting others walk all over you. It is important to stay calm, but also to stand up to a bully who would try to take all the credit. Modest redress of any unfairness will meet with success.

◗ If your final throw brings three moon coins: do not confuse modesty and weakness. Get on quietly with the task of putting everything in order, even if this causes friction with someone else. Don't take offence, but set about improvements, even if this means bringing someone down a peg or two! Success comes from wise behaviour and willingness to reform. Good fortune comes to the person who achieves important results without seeking too much attention.

16 The band

This forecast, composed of Earth and Thunder, has special significance if you are a mother (Earth), or an eldest son (Thunder). This would suggest a moment of peak importance in your life.

Success comes from enthusiasm and creativity in a group activity. This reading celebrates the power of working together for something creative in a small group, where one dominant or charismatic person can spark an enthusiastic response among others. Whether you see yourself as the leader of the group, or recognize that this role needs to be taken by another, the moment is definitely ripe to bring together a group of people to achieve a result. Unity is the key: but so is action. Something must be undertaken, such as an event organized, or a job initiated. One person, with great strength and originality, can lead the others to brilliance. This is the moment to employ, rather than be employed; a time for action, not for waiting. It is important that there is willingness, and a shared spirit, among all members of the group, who can then act like a band or orchestra and create beautiful music together. Each person has a task of individual merit and worth, but it is only through their combined energies that the beauty of the undertaking appears. All aims must have group appeal, and all efforts for achievement must have a united purpose. A leader may emerge who is spirited, and has presence; but the work of every person is vital to the success of the project. The most important ingredient for success in any venture now is enthusiasm: make sure that all members of a group connected with your ambitions are equally enthused, and that no feelings of opposition exist between individuals. Then, success really comes from good energy and organization. This reading is connected with the beginning of summer, when thunderstorms have vast energy; here, the thunder charges the atmosphere and refreshes a dull situation with new ideas.

The moving lines

If any of your throws produced three identical coins (suns or moons), this is called a moving line. Read the relevant line(s) below, then change the line(s) to the opposite symbol, and look up and read the new forecast (see pages 44–5). Don't forget that your tablet of throws is written from the bottom up, so your first throw is the bottom one.

◗ If the first throw brought all moon coins: enthusiasm for its own sake is not helpful. One individual must not become self-important or egotistical, but must work with others to obtain a response that will bring success.

◗ If the second throw was all moon coins: this celebrates one person who remains focused and firm about the desired goal. Neither overrating people 'above', nor undervaluing those 'below', this cheerful group member treats all equally and helps to keep the momentum going so that, with perseverance, good fortune is certain. Some self-reliance would be an asset.

◗ If the third throw produced all moon coins: this is not a time to hesitate for too long. It is possible that delay can result in a lost opportunity, and the chance will later be viewed as a crucial moment that was wasted.

● If the fourth throw produced all sun coins: you are unquestionably the able leader whose charismatic powers can move mountains and create powerful fellow feeling. You propel others into action and enthuse them with a creative aim, which will succeed as long as you pull together.

◯ If the fifth throw produced all moon coins: you may feel too pressured, wondering how you can continue with such a burden. And yet, the pressures placed on you have a positive effect too, as they keep you focused and make you determined to get through it. With such a load, tight organization is the way to succeed.

◯ If your final throw produced all moon coins: you may have become too enthusiastic about a project that was never a reality, and you may be feeling cheated and silly. However, if this leads to a realization, your course will change with positive results. Do not blame yourself, but be willing to recognize the moment when such a goal may be deluded; then something valuable will come from your clarity.

17 Take a break

This forecast is made up of Thunder and Lake, so has more significance if you are an eldest son (Thunder), or a third or youngest daughter (Lake). This then indicates a moment of prime concern and importance for you.

Rest and recuperation are in order. Thunder may crouch in the earth and rest, waiting like a sleeping tiger. Here, the image is of thunder resting in a lake, as it may do in winter. It is important for you to follow suit, to create some time to cease activity and recover your energy. Without any accusations of laziness or too much inactivity, it is sometimes vital to recharge our batteries in order to use them with more clarity and focus for the future. Without rest, the mind cannot see properly; without relaxation, the body cannot work efficiently. So if this is your reading, don't risk further action if you are exhausted or mentally and emotionally stressed. It may be a good idea to make a journey across the lake – quite literally, to go away over water or by water – even if only for a weekend, to put some distance between you and your affairs, in order to see everything in perspective. Be ready to follow the lead of someone gentle and unhurried, whose priorities may be different from your own. Don't worry about taking a break now: until you are less jaded, the moment is not ripe for tackling any activities that demand physical or mental exertion. It is as though night has fallen, forcing someone who has been working relentlessly to stop for a moment and consider. If you don't rest now, damage may be done – not only to your personal health, but also to a future event. Be prepared, too, to let others assume the lead and do the worrying, while you step back, have a break, and view all the possible options for the future.

17

The moving lines

If any of your throws produced three identical coins (suns or moons), this is called a moving line. Read the relevant line(s) below, then change the line(s) to the opposite symbol, and look up and read the new forecast (see pages 44–5). Don't forget that your tablet of throws is written from the bottom up, so your first throw is the bottom one.

● If your first throw resulted in all sun coins: be ready to listen to the advice of others, even if their standards or interests are different from your own. It would be wise now to hear what others have to say, although it may not be necessary to follow their advice. Be open and relaxed to other approaches, and to someone else taking the lead for a while.

☽ If your second throw was all moon coins: it is important to look carefully at the people with whom you associate. Don't make the mistake of befriending someone who is less thoughtful and intelligent than you. Choose your friends carefully.

☽ If your third throw produced all moon coins: this may be the moment to let go of friends who are holding you back. It is important to listen to wise advice from someone you respect; to do this, it may be necessary to go away to a retreat of some kind. Don't be afraid to let go of the past. You can't choose all the options, so select your future path and ideas carefully.

● If your fourth throw is all suns: be sure to distinguish between good friends and advisors, and those who simply flatter you. An honest friend may be one who disagrees with you: you are faced with a test of your ego now, and you need to make sensible choices rather than depending on hangers-on.

● If your fifth throw shows all sun coins: this demonstrates sincerity in your actions, and the probability that you are following a wise personal path. Success comes to you!

◗ If your final throw is all moons: you are unselfish in your attentions. Your own work may be finished, and you may have found a sort of wisdom, and a new delight in life. But even if you would prefer to be a loner, with time for your own spiritual or intellectual pursuits, you are prepared to help another person in their time of need. Unselfishly you give, and as a result you will gain something more special than riches.

18 The phoenix rises

This forecast, being made up of Wind and Mountain, has special significance if you are the eldest daughter (Wind), or a third or younger son (Mountain).

Make up for lost time! This reading tells us that there has been disaster in the recent past; many opportunities have been wasted through apathy or uncaring indifference. However, this leads to a chance for new growth, and the opportunity to put time or effort to better use in the future. If this is your reading, it is now within your control to remedy much of the lost time. The key is to work on something that has not been completed, or has been let go, such as a partially finished education or a dilapidated house. Out of the ashes of past destruction or mistakes, a new and positive future can emerge. This is an invitation to rise like a phoenix from the ashes – to refuse to cry over past mistakes, but to turn things around and work for a healthy and prosperous future. There may be difficulty or danger in any undertaking at the moment; but it is important not to give in. Deliberate very carefully: it may be wise to take three days to consider what actions would be in everyone's best interests. Look at the past and present damage, and think carefully about the best way forward, without rushing straight in. A trip may be necessary to further your affairs; action must now take over from previous inaction or carelessness. This is the time to learn from past mistakes, decide what caused them, and rise anew from them – literally out of the old ashes. There is even a hint of reform associated with this forecast. You may have to tackle a situation of previous wrongdoing and corruption, and to correct matters if injustices have occurred in the past. Be ready to whip into action those around you who have previously been uncommitted or unconcerned with important issues that affect everyone: changes are heralded!

18

The moving lines

If any of your throws produced three identical coins (suns or moons), this is called a moving line. Read the relevant line(s) below, then change the line(s) to the opposite symbol, and look up and read the new forecast (see pages 44–5). Don't forget that your tablet of throws is written from the bottom up, so your first throw is the bottom one.

◯ If your first throw was all moon coins: present circumstances are the result of too much reliance on an out-of-date approach. You need to reassess your present life and adjust the way you do things. There are possible pitfalls in finding a new way forward; but if you consider carefully before you act, all augurs well for a successful outcome.

● If your second throw resulted in three sun coins: a mistake has been made by someone who didn't have enough knowledge or education to avoid it. Don't be offensive or cruel, but it's important to find a better way to proceed in the future. Gentleness and discretion are called for.

● If your third throw produced all sun coins: if you attempt to make radical reforms too hastily, you will only create tensions and problems with others. Try to proceed with tact, and address issues that concern you with care; but it is important to tackle these problems, and don't worry too much about ruffling some feathers if this is ultimately required. Be diplomatic.

◗ If your fourth throw produced all moon coins: if you are unwilling to make changes in the present, and continue on a course from the past, matters will steadily worsen. You must avoid a stalemate from continuing.

◗ If your fifth throw produced all moon coins: you may have inherited a difficult state of affairs produced by the poor judgement of someone in the past. You cannot repair the damage alone but, with assistance, much can be put right.

● If your final throw produced all sun coins: don't sit back and criticize the mistakes of people around you who are in the front line. If problems exist which are created by governments or bosses or organized bodies, be prepared to get involved to make a difference. Even if you stay out of the principal line of argument between others, be prepared to express a view of what is right, in a gentle and cogent form. Be ready to contribute to changes for the better.

19 The little candle

Composed of Lake and Earth, this reading is of greater impact if you are either a third or youngest daughter (Lake), or a mother (Earth). If so, you are arriving at a very significant moment in your life.

Success comes from modest beginnings. The meaning of this forecast is complex and it can be read on many levels. Overall, it can be seen as an omen of success on a grand scale, but there are aspects of life now that need to be handled with care and thought. This forecast is directly related to the period straight after the Winter Solstice, when the light begins to grow stronger. The light of the two suns at the bottom of the pictogram spreads upwards, indicating the gradual increase of power and light, with success even from modest beginnings. Just as the moment after the Solstice gradually highlights the joyous approach of spring, so, too, your personal weathering of past storms and darker days may be replaced by growth, success and progress. However, there are tasks to perform in spring, in order to make best use of all that is budding and alive. It is a moment of intense energy and commitment to capitalize on all the positive aspects of the time. This is the season to plant – so if you have jobs that need doing and ambitions that need launching, this is the most opportune time to do so. Any seeds you sow now can grow, but your projects must be attacked with energy and hard work. The most beautiful dreams can become reality with nurture. This reading has another name: Approach – think of this as a challenge to approach what is dearest to you steadily. Like a little candle that nevertheless burns evenly and well, illumination can come from the tiniest source. It's also important to look after people who depend on you, such as children, or those who work for you. Success is destined: but this is still no time for personal arrogance. The gentlest words will have the most lasting effect.

19

The moving lines

If any of your throws produced three identical coins (suns or moons), this is called a moving line. Read the relevant line(s) below, then change the line(s) to the opposite symbol, and look up and read the new forecast (see pages 44–5). Don't forget that your tablet of throws is written from the bottom up, so your first throw is the bottom one.

● If your first throw produced all sun coins: now is the time to persevere with important goals. You will find help in high places – those with influence are in a position to give you much practical help. Work with integrity will truly prosper now; if you have real abilities, these will come to the fore where it matters.

● If your second throw produced three sun coins: it is important to be consistent in your behaviour, and to act without anger or fear. You will certainly need to have personal staying power to see your wishes through, but this you seem to have.

◗ If your third throw produced all moon coins: everything is going very well for you now, but this is no time to rest on your laurels. Be very considerate to all around you while you pursue your dreams, and be ready to accept responsibilities graciously.

◗ If your fourth throw resulted in all moon coins: bravery – in terms of asking for help from someone in a position of authority and respect – will pay dividends. Even the most successful or celebrated person is available to you at this time, if your attitude is cheerful and you are well prepared. All signs for progress are favourable.

◗ If your fifth throw produced three moon coins: you are certain to meet with someone in power or authority whom you may admire, and who will understand the wisdom of your ideas. You may feel you are mixing with someone superior to you in either education or position, but all works out well for all concerned.

◗ If your sixth and final throw results in three moon coins: you may have finished some work and become free from responsibility, but it is likely that you could make a considerable difference to someone's life if you were available to help. Good fortune comes to everyone from your generous use of time.

20 The tower on the hill

This forecast is made up of Earth and Wind, so has special significance if you are either a mother (Earth) or the eldest daughter (Wind). In this case, you are entering a moment of particular importance and with far-reaching consequences.

Success comes from sincerity and consideration. This forecast is connected with the early autumn, when the light begins to wane, and when things wind to a close and new plans should be made. The reading suggests a test of character. When you look out from a high hill or a watchtower you can see for many miles, and everything takes on a new perspective from this objective position. Equally, a watchtower or beacon can be seen for miles around, making a landmark for those below. Thus, in this reading, you are both watching and being watched. You must consider carefully what you want to do, looking with insight and deep personal contemplation at the aims you have set yourself, considering their overall importance and the merit of the undertaking or scheme. But remember, you are also being watched by others: they will look to see how you proceed, how you handle the work and responsibilities before you, and how you behave overall. If you are sincere in your thoughts and actions, success will come for your goals and ideals now. If you are only playing out a role to be observed, and it is only for show, and lacks real heart or commitment, you will be exposed and seen through. You must judge your own actions, and be ready to be judged in turn for what you do. If there is real truth and integrity — an earnest wish to make a difference and contribute something better in life — you will certainly succeed. If there is a superficiality, or even lack of sincerity, in your aims, you must be prepared to fall flat. You are in a position to make an impact — like a teacher. Do not abuse your power!

20

The moving lines

If any of your throws produced three identical coins (suns or moons), this is called a moving line. Read the relevant line(s) below, then change the line(s) to the opposite symbol, and look up and read the new forecast (see pages 44–5). Don't forget that your tablet of throws is written from the bottom up, so your first throw is the bottom one.

◐ If your first throw produces all moon coins: look very deeply at the affairs around you, and be careful not to make shallow judgements, or place too much importance on appearances. This is a moment for wisdom. Do not overlook something precious, which lies at your feet!

◐ If your second throw produces all moon coins: be careful not to limit your understanding of affairs right now. There is a danger of making a false guess because you are only considering a limited range of information. Be prepared to widen your view, and become more objective.

◐ If your third throw is all moons: this is a very important throw, as it suggests personal transformation. You are contemplating your own actions, looking deeply inwards, and are ready to admit any shortcomings. This is the moment of truth, when you may find the courage to change a habit or alter your opinion, being aware that such a change was necessary. Thus, from such inner reflection, good fortune will come.

◗ When your fourth throw results in all moon coins: you have excellent instincts about how to improve conditions around you – either in your personal affairs, or in business. Either way, your advice is good, and you should be ready to express your thoughts and perceptions without arrogance, but with clarity.

● If your fifth throw produced all sun coins: you must be ready to reconsider your actions and proposed plans, by first considering why you want to pursue them. You are in a position of respect, and others admire you: so it is important to understand your own motives and impulses well. If the impact you wish to have around you is positive, you can relax, knowing you are not mistaken in your goals.

● If your final throw is all suns: you have reached a plateau of personal wisdom. You are ready to look inwards, and to understand your situation very unselfishly. For the moment, at least, your ego is set to one side, so you achieve happiness and a feeling of deep personal peace.

21 Clearing obstacles

This forecast is made up of Thunder and Fire, so has extra significance if you are either an eldest son (Thunder), or a second-born daughter (Fire). This would then suggest that you are entering a time of peak importance.

Success comes through justice and arbitration. This reading can be understood from the metaphor of the cleansing power of thunder and lightning: a powerful electrical storm dispels tensions in the atmosphere, a clearing that takes energy and determination. Nature is provoked by the build-up of elements and responds with a storm. In the same way, it may take a metaphoric 'thunderclap' to deal with tensions that have arisen in life. This reading is strongly connected with law and the possibility of lawsuits, which are necessary to sweep away a series of tensions and injustices. It suggests that it is in your interest now to let the law play a part in dealing with something that has become obstructive in your life. There is definitely an issue or problem in your way, and it will serve you well to place your faith in justice. The balance between thunder and lightning is positive: the two work together to dispel pressures. As such, you can expect an overly tense situation now to be resolved through fair-mindedness and the clear expression of these pent-up frustrations. Be prepared, however, to be vigorous and put some real energy and effort into your undertaking. It is important to go after your desired outcome without venom or violence, but equally without being weak-willed. The more reasonable your behaviour, the more certain you can be of success and achieving the aim you have. Neither should you take matters into your own hands: be prepared to submit to an outside adjudicator, who will advise you fairly and award the right decision. You are set to break through some barriers that have held you back, and from here on your direction will be altered considerably.

21

The moving lines

If any of your throws produced three identical coins (suns or moons), this is called a moving line. Read the relevant line(s) below, then change the line(s) to the opposite symbol, and look up and read the new forecast (see pages 44–5). Don't forget that your tablet of throws is written from the bottom up, so your first throw is the bottom one.

● If your first throw produced all sun coins: you may need to re-think your position, and be prepared to alter your intended direction. Look closely at whether there is any fault in what you propose. Be careful, too, to stay within the 'rules'; but if you have done something which you know needs to be remedied, you can submit to a higher source, and you will come through with only a small penalty. Address any misdemeanour now, before it grows out of proportion!

◑ If your second throw was all moons: don't lose your sense of balance and become too angry over the actions of another person. You are in danger of making a mountain out of a molehill: although someone has transgressed and behaved with neglect, it is important to keep things in proportion. Then, all will go well for you.

◑ If your third throw produces all moon coins: someone who has let you down is going to be given only a light dressing down, for the person who will decide the outcome is inexperienced and over-lenient. However, the important thing for you is to remain focused about the future and not to waste energy over what is past. Move on.

● If your fourth throw results in three sun coins: it will take some courage to address something you see as an injustice now, as someone with real authority and standing seems to be at fault. Even if you think your chances of getting fair treatment are slim, be ready to put in some genuine effort, and you will in fact succeed.

◐ When your fifth throw produces all moon coins: you may be taking on a responsibility that demands much dedication and even has some unattractive dangers attached. But be strong! By being aware of the difficulties, but not overawed by them, you will avoid any mistakes and succeed.

● When your sixth and final throw produces all sun coins: here is a warning not to allow bad habits or errors to pile up. If you find yourself accumulating problems through lack of sense or bad management, they can ultimately cause a disaster. Deal with something small now, before it threatens your peace.

22 Volcano in the snow

This reading is composed of Fire and Mountain, so has special significance if you are either the second daughter (Fire), or the youngest son (Mountain). This would suggest a period of peak importance occurring in your life.

Create a balance between beauty and the intellect. The image is drawn from the metaphor of a fire blazing out of the earth and illuminating a great mountain. Like fire in the snow, there is grace and beauty in this contrast of opposites, which creates a union from disparate things. This reading is strongly concerned with the light-hearted aspect of beautifying yourself and your surroundings. But it's important to do this in balance with the serious issues in life that require thought, energy and attention. It's wonderful to decorate your home, for this adds to your feeling of wellbeing as well as giving aesthetic pleasure; but it's even more important to make sure that the structure itself is safe and secure before you turn your attention to the details. If too little attention is given to the look of your surroundings, there is a lack of balance and beauty; if too much is given to it, other important issues will be neglected. Try to create a balance, then, between what is worthy of adornment, and what is needed from your intellect, your physical energy and practical issues. There is beauty in the fire coming from the volcano in the snowy landscape, but it has power only over a limited field. It is right to spend time and effort making small details perfect; but they will not make up for a shortfall in material necessities. It is still important to look at the serious side of life, and this may be especially true between people. If your question concerns a relationship, don't place too much reliance on appearances alone. Make sure there is a bond between souls and minds, as well as physical attraction.

22

The moving lines

If any of your throws produced three identical coins (suns or moons), this is called a moving line. Read the relevant line(s) below, then change the line(s) to the opposite symbol, and look up and read the new forecast (see pages 44–5). Don't forget that your tablet of throws is written from the bottom up, so your first throw is the bottom one.

● If your first throw produced all sun coins: you are just starting out on a new road, and it is important that you are noticed for your own merits. Real ability and energy will be understood. You must prepare for a long period of study and preparation to gain the very worthy ends you seek.

◗ If your second throw produced three moon coins: the decorative impression of something is lovely, but the true value lies in the real person or matter behind it. Look deeply at someone or something before you judge its worth.

● If your third throw is all suns: it is good and quite right to enjoy the moment and the beauty of the occasion. However, there is a danger that this may distract you from your path. Like strong wine at lunchtime, there is pleasure in the moment, but a need to return to work afterwards! Perseverance is crucial.

◗ If your fourth throw produced all moon coins: here is a choice between two things, one of which is straightforward and simple, the other more elegant and outwardly beautiful. This time, you are urged not to overlook the person or situation of value in favour of the obviously pretty option. The simpler person, or direction, or item, is the one that possesses the true grace.

◗ If your fifth throw produced all moon coins: don't be concerned if you are unable to compete with others in the beauty of your clothes or your home. Though your home may be smaller or your clothes simpler, your heart and mind have the most to offer, and will be appreciated truly for their worth.

● If your final throw produced all sun coins: all is revealed when you reach the peak of the mountain. You are now able to see that it is your substance, and not your appearance, which is valued. Equally, decoration is no longer so important, and embellishment does not conceal the shape within. You look beyond the superficial, and are successful in your approach. Good fortune comes.

23 Raising the roof

Composed of Earth and Mountain, this reading has greater significance if you are a mother (Earth), or a third or subsequent son (Mountain). In either case, you are entering a period of peak importance.

Success comes from firm foundations. The image of this forecast is of a house whose roof is not properly supported from underneath, so is liable to collapse. This suggests the time is not ripe for you to undertake a new venture, as it is not properly prepared. You may not yet have enough information, or are perhaps relying on people who are unsupportive or have no staying power. So, the only thing to do is to concentrate on putting your own house in order; if you expect much of others you will be disappointed. This is not a good time for change, so put up with the situation for the moment. You should also consider whether you may be expecting too much of yourself, without having enough support from others. If you try to raise the roof of a house without the walls on which it must rest being secure, the roof will collapse. So look carefully at your plans, and consider whether everything is in place to support you. If you find that either your team, or others you must deal with, are lacking in will or ability, wait! Make sure you are completely ready yourself. Be willing to learn a little more, or take a little longer, and don't just jump in with high hopes. Building this house, even metaphorically, is a considerable project: it is the shelter of your hopes, dreams and needs; and it is an investment of your time and resources. Take care to construct your dreams very slowly and carefully, and treat those whom you may need to depend on later with care and good feeling . Raise your roof gradually, and make certain you have everything in place before you do so. Until then, there is still much work to do, and some waiting to endure.

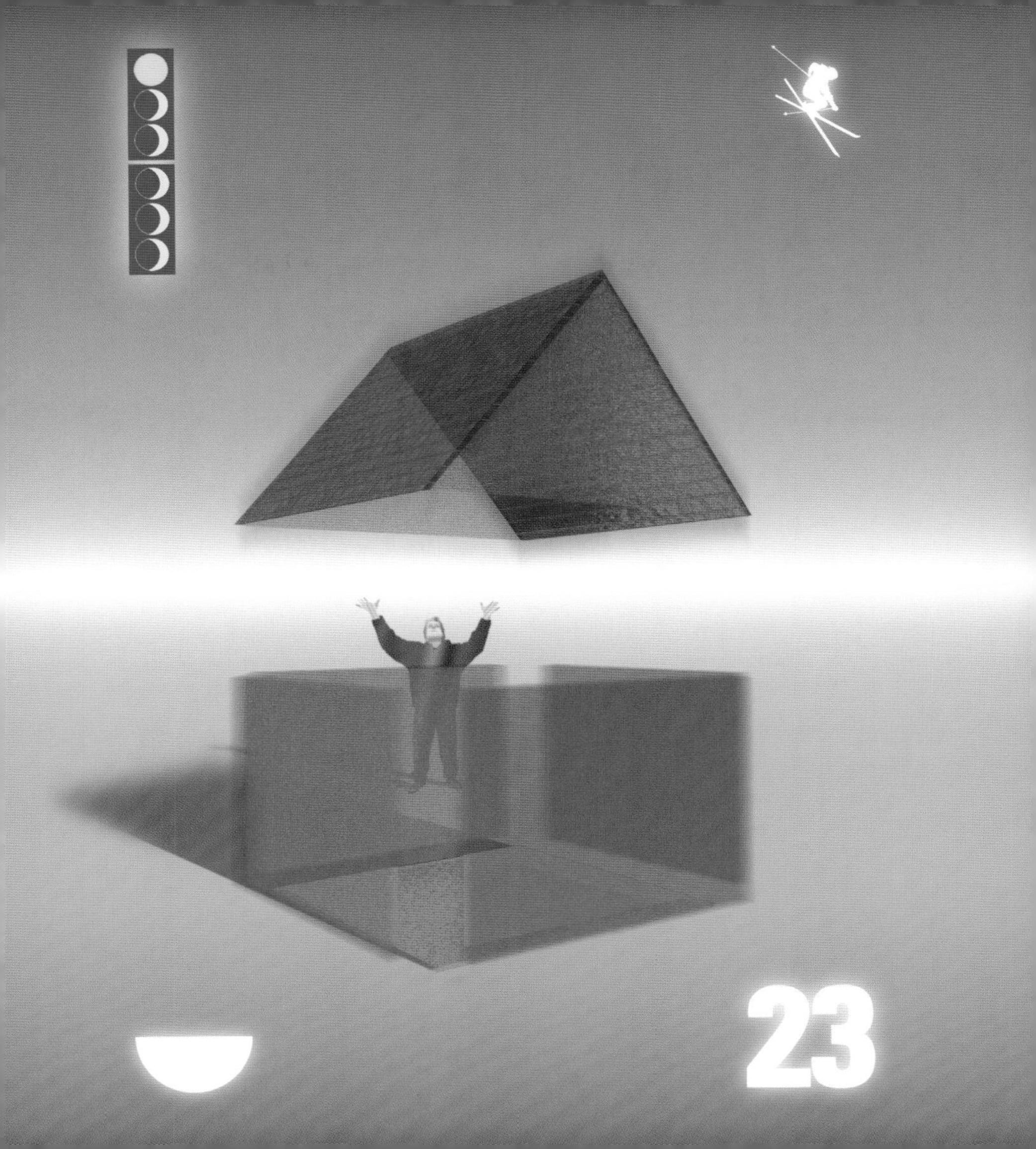
23

The moving lines

If any of your throws produced three identical coins (suns or moons), this is called a moving line. Read the relevant line(s) below, then change the line(s) to the opposite symbol, and look up and read the new forecast (see pages 44–5). Don't forget that your tablet of throws is written from the bottom up, so your first throw is the bottom one.

◯ If the first throw produced all moon coins: your fine intelligence is no help against a gaggle of people with inferior abilities, who make their way forwards despite obvious failings. Use your wisdom, then, to wait it out; and do not rail against what is temporarily inevitable. If you clash with them, you will only injure yourself more.

◯ If the second throw produced all moon coins: it is of no use to stick stubbornly to your own viewpoint, as there are too many people around you who will undermine your ideas. Again, it is not the moment to move forward. Waiting will inevitably frustrate you, and yet there is little point in fighting. Save your strength for another day, when it will have greater impact.

◯ If your third throw was all moon coins: it may now be necessary to break free from other people whose ideas and attitudes differ vastly from your own. No gain comes from rubbing against the grain, so it is better to retreat and spend time alone. However, you must do this discreetly, trying not to worsen any feelings of enmity.

◗ If your fourth throw resulted in all moon coins: an error is clear, and a new route must be found. This may mean starting all over again, but persisting in the current course would only bring misfortune and disappointment.

◗ If your fifth throw presented all moon coins: the start of the project or venture has been undermined by weak direction, but there is an end to this in sight. Now, guidance comes from a stronger personality to whom all concerned will listen. Your waiting time is almost over, and the roof is nearly in place. Good shelter is imminent.

● If your sixth and final throw produced all sun coins: good times can now return. The worth of your own sense and ability has been demonstrated and observed, and someone who has had too much influence and little ability loses their position, or leaves the project. Your patience has been a credit to you, and the feeling of frustration now fades. All is well.

24 A fresh start

This forecast is made up of Thunder and Earth, so has extra weight if you are either an eldest son (Thunder), or a mother (Earth). In either case, you are entering a time of heightened importance.

Great success comes from allowing nature to take its course. This reading corresponds to the time of the Winter Solstice itself (December 21 in the Northern Hemisphere). This is a turning point, the moment at which light begins to return after the long days of darkness. The recent past may have included difficulties and obstacles, or a feeling of hopelessness or drudgery, but this is now coming to an end, and the whole positive cycle of life begins anew. These changes do not come from a revolution, but from a natural process – night succeeds day, and day night. And so there is a gentle transformation, with lasting results and a glowing future. You are now surrounded by all manner of success, but don't hurry things unnecessarily. Impatience now would be misplaced. Thunder stirs in the earth, like the force of life waiting to return. But it is very important not to attempt to hasten this activity, and to let it take its own course of time. There is a moment of necessary rest at the time of the Winter Solstice, when energy grows but must not be dissipated. So it is for you, if this is your reading; like someone returning gradually from poor health to full vitality, let nature undertake the gentle process of moving you forward, and be cheerful and optimistic that the return is definitely coming. After what feels like a long winter, signs are clear that healing is occurring. Yet careful nurturing is still required. For example, it takes time to rebuild confidence between two people after a serious quarrel: too much strain, too early, can reverse the process of recovery. Declare a short period of holiday: enjoy the resting time, and don't fight it. Be optimistic at the signs given by nature, and be ready to dance on the fast-approaching, first truly spring-like day.

24

The moving lines

If any of your throws produced three identical coins (suns or moons), this is called a moving line. Read the relevant line(s) below, then change the line(s) to the opposite symbol, and look up and read the new forecast (see pages 44–5). Don't forget that your tablet of throws is written from the bottom up, so your first throw is the bottom one.

● If your first throw produced all sun coins: you may have taken a slight detour from your important path; but you have discovered in time, and no harm is done. Do not be too hard on yourself, but be ready to retrace your steps without argument or attributing blame to anyone.

◗ If your second throw produces all moon coins: it would be wise to allow someone whom you respect to influence your direction. You may need to start again on an important task, but you will have good company for the journey, and good friendship while you work.

◗ If your third throw produces all moon coins: it would be a mistake now to start a task you want to fulfil over and over again. One false start has no harm attached, and yet too many beginnings suggest weak determination, or bad planning. Make sure you know what you want, and where you are headed, before expending more energy on too many diverse plans.

○ If your fourth throw is all moon coins: don't be worried if your ideas separate you from the crowd. In this situation, you have a strong sense of intuition, and should be guided by your own ideas and wishes. Don't be afraid to strike out on a new path away from someone who has a different set of values or outlook.

○ If your fifth throw results in all moon coins: it takes strength of character to admit taking a wrong course of action. If this is what you are now aware of, you will gain nothing but praise and respect from your friends and associates when you admit that change is required. A previously poor decision is mended by an honest assessment of it, and the nobility either to say 'sorry', or to change the way forward. From either course, only good will come.

○ If your sixth and final throw produces all moon coins: there is a path ahead that will lead to misfortune if you miss the right moment to turn around. Either a stubborn attitude which is based on wrong information, or being out of step with others and with the times, will cause you harm in the future. Look clearly at the signs, and if a new way of behaviour is called for, pay attention to this before it really is too late.

25 On the right track

This forecast is composed of Thunder and Sky, so has even more impact for you if you are an eldest son (Thunder), or a father (Sky) – or both. In either of these cases, this suggests a period of peak importance is unfolding.

A moment of heavenly protection. This reading is very positive: it tells us that we are on the right path – our instincts are good and true, and we are guided by our spirit, which is contemplative and innocent. If this is your reading, you have heavenly protection at this moment. Within each person is the seed of something divine – the striving spirit of goodness and deity; and it is attention and devotion to this inner god-like quality that is so powerful for you now. It leads you unwaveringly to a course of innocent good purpose; your instincts and inner voice are clear and true. You are not looking for personal gain, nor are you motivated by rewards other than personal growth and the expansion of spirit and mind. Your instincts will lead you to success in your path, and you will be willing and ready to persevere to achieve your personal goal. You have found a balance between instinct and reflection – the kind of contemplation that goes along with quick intuitive thought. You feel a divine inspiration – perhaps from nature, or music, or inner being. You may also experience a state of child-like joy, of innocence, and of renewed energy and vitality. Almost unexpectedly, you come to the truths that are important to your code of living. You survive all minor setbacks, because your inner strength and lightness of being are assured. Selfishness doesn't seem to threaten you: your mind and heart are pure, and you will show outwardly this same peace and goodness that is in your inner self. Good fortune comes to you now.

25

The moving lines

If any of your throws produced three identical coins (suns or moons), this is called a moving line. Read the relevant line(s) below, then change the line(s) to the opposite symbol, and look up and read the new forecast (see pages 44–5). Don't forget that your tablet of throws is written from the bottom up, so your first throw is the bottom one.

● If your first throw produced all sun coins: the first impulses of your heart and soul are good. Follow what your instincts dictate now, and good fortune will follow.

◗ If your second throw produces all moon coins: it is important now to attend to your responsibilities for their own sake – whether it be arduous duty, or necessary work, or meditative thought. Joy should be sought in the doing, rather than in the anticipated results. Unexpected pleasure can come from simply doing the job well.

◗ If your third throw produces all moon coins: sometimes, actions go against us that are not in our control. You may now be the victim of an unfair act, but it is essential to cope with this without becoming frantic. Go with the demands of the moment, and take your strength from within.

● If your fourth throw produces all sun coins: if something really belongs to you, it cannot be lost. This may be helpful in terms of a relationship: if there truly is a bond with another person, no one can steal this from you. Be calm, put anxieties to one side, and be true to your own conscience. Avoid the chance of being upset or misled by other people now.

● If your fifth throw results in all sun coins: if you accidentally become the victim of another's mistake, don't try to resolve it by taking action yourself. In this instance nature should be allowed to run its course, and healing will occur if you are not to blame. Improvements will come eventually, but allow them to do so naturally, without inflaming the situation.

● If your sixth and final throw results in all sun coins: there are moments when your own innocent inspirations and wishes go against the grain. Nothing will be gained by pushing too hard to achieve your ends. Now is such a time: the moment is inopportune, so you must be prepared to wait until the clouds disperse and rain no longer threatens. Allow fate to have its hand for the moment.

26 Hidden treasure

This forecast is composed of Sky and Mountain, so has even more impact for you if you are either a father (Sky), or the third or younger son (Mountain) – or both. In any of these cases, a moment of peak importance is unfolding.

A forecast with hidden inner meanings. This is a complex reading, with three different meanings associated with its imagery of sky and mountain. Firstly, heaven within the mountain: an awareness that what is precious is worth holding onto. The mountain contains hidden treasure – the gifts of nature herself, such as gold and gems. In a relationship, this suggests the desirability of staying close to someone. Strength and clarity of mind are necessary, as are a soft heart and a strong will. In the second meaning, the mountain is trying to hold back the power of heaven. One or two people are holding back the wishes of someone more powerful or wealthy, but lacking clarity or sense. They succeed, and everyone is better off for their restraining actions. In the third meaning, mountain and sky cling powerfully together, an ideal balance. The wise soul will look within and discover the strength of the mountain married to the creative spark from heaven: in other words, inspiration. It would be greatly to your advantage to set off in pursuit of a very important goal now. Travel is certainly indicated, and success comes from well-laid plans. If this is your reading, you must assess which of the three interpretations is most applicable to your situation. Look back over the recent past; take note of any 'hidden treasure' that may have been overlooked. Knowledge must be sought and actively used. Whichever interpretation most applies to you, there will certainly be an adjustment to be made between someone of power and influence, and someone of less power. Once this adjustment has been made, all will be well and success will come.

26

The moving lines

If any of your throws produced three identical coins (suns or moons), this is called a moving line. Read the relevant line(s) below, then change the line(s) to the opposite symbol, and look up and read the new forecast (see pages 44–5). Don't forget that your tablet of throws is written from the bottom up, so your first throw is the bottom one.

● If your first throw produced all sun coins: this is definitely not the right time to try to force any changes or forward progress. Circumstances themselves must first change and this has not yet happened so, to alter a current situation to your advantage, wait with patience and watch for an opportunity that will come in due course.

● If your second throw was all sun coins: there is a conflict between wishing for movement and change, and being aware that the time is premature for any vigorous attempts to effect that change. Sitting it out may not be so difficult, as you are perfectly aware that something further needs to take place before a journey or action can be justified. This, incidentally, allows more time for preparation for a time when it will be possible to move towards the result you desire.

● If the third throw produced all sun coins: now the path begins to clear for a move forward, for a new direction to be embarked on. There are still problems to negotiate, but a respectful awareness of the difficulties will help you, and it is right, now, to set out after a purpose. Be attentive, and stick closely to your goal.

◗ If the fourth throw was all moon coins: you must watch a person with power and influence now, but you can do this very effectively. Foreseeing future difficulties as a possibility, the steps you take now to prevent later problems are the right ones, and success comes instead of difficulty.

◗ If the fifth throw resulted in all moon coins: here again you need to thwart a wrong choice or misuse of power by someone close to you; in this instance, it can be achieved most effectively by going at it by indirect means. Don't try to strike out directly and create a clash of wills: be tactful in the way you handle the other person. You will be successful if you can find a way to make them think they are changing course of their own volition!

● If your sixth and final throw resulted in all sun coins: all obstructions and complications now shift, and a way is found to go forward in pursuit of a truly important personal desire. Whoever has stood in your way, or has been opposed to your choice, now relents, and your wishes are achieved.

27 A laughing smile

This forecast, being made up of Thunder and Mountain, will have even more impact if you are either an eldest son (Thunder) or the third or younger (Mountain). In both cases this suggests you are entering a key period.

To find your true vocation brings success. The image behind this forecast is of a mouth in the act of both eating and laughing. The reading concerns the nourishment, therefore, of both body and soul. All ventures that will bring nourishment, and make provision for the future, are indicated; but there is also an emphasis on happiness and fun. It's always necessary to feed the family, but it's just as important to find a way to do this that will be of benefit to soul and mind. So, if this is your reading, you must urgently decide how you want to nurture yourself: how to find a healthy, happy way to fulfil your career wishes that at the same time satisfies the soul as much as mind and body. Consider deeply whether the work you propose to take on will bring real joy in the doing of it. Another thing to remember is that those for whom you take responsibility must also be fed: you must ensure that efforts are neither wasted nor unappreciated by anyone you care for. If some responsibilities are not reciprocated, then unfair advantage may be taken of you, causing resentment. Consider whether you can justify the responsibility for another person that you are committing yourself to. Think very carefully of all that passes your lips: food, drink, laughter, words. Be kind, gentle, attentive, and moderate. The object for which you are striving should involve harmony and balance in work and play, a healthy lifestyle and joy in your daily life. This sums up a true sense of vocation, and true nourishment in every sense. This reading is also connected with spring; fruition can be expected at this time, and the reading will become even more relevant.

27

The moving lines

If any of your throws produced three identical coins (suns or moons), this is called a moving line. Read the relevant line(s) below, then change the line(s) to the opposite symbol, and look up and read the new forecast (see pages 44–5). Don't forget that your tablet of throws is written from the bottom up, so your first throw is the bottom one.

● If your first throw produces all sun coins: there is tension and difficulty ahead if you allow yourself to become attached or drawn to what other people have, as opposed to what you truly need. You are almost magically protected, with huge self-reliance; but you need not judge yourself by other people's standards or their need for trappings. Be content with what is true to you, and don't become envious or diverted.

◗ If your second throw results in all moon coins: this throw is an admonition to someone who is not working hard enough to provide his or her own support. There are times when it is necessary to be helped by others, but it is not an ideal situation indefinitely. It is now time to consider the importance of your own contributions to your future, and take steps to become more independent again.

◗ If your third throw produces all moon coins: you are not taking care of your health, and to continue on this path will bring terrible consequences. Look after yourself at once! Eat well and in balance, and work sensibly, before you burn out!

◗ If your fourth throw produces all moon coins: you will be very lucky in business, because your chosen path seems to be for the benefit for many people beside yourself. You have a high-minded attitude to work and understand the importance of putting your energies into something worthwhile, which helps others. Choosing the right people to work with you could be a huge boost to your ambitions and ideas. Look for them extremely carefully.

◗ If your fifth throw has resulted in all moon coins: this is a good moment to seek advice from someone who is an expert in their field. This person can help you find the best way to fulfil obligations to yourself and to others, connected with your work and vocational path. It is important to be resolved about how and what you aim to do, and to stick closely with that decision: then, everything will prosper.

● If your sixth and final throw is all sun coins: you have taken on a great responsibility, but you will thrive with it and fulfil the demands you have made on yourself. You must be the initiator, the one who takes action; as long as you understand the weight of the burden on you, and assume it knowingly, you will prosper.

28 Overload

This reading is made up of Wind and Lake, so has even greater significance for you if you are either the eldest daughter (Wind), or the third or younger (Lake). It would suggest you are coming to a key moment in your life.

A warning to slow down! This reading serves as a warning that your life is out of balance: you are asking too much of yourself, emotionally, physically and intellectually. The suggestion is certainly not that doom will follow, but it is very important now to shift the balance before the weight of life overtakes you. For some time, perhaps, you have been accumulating too much responsibility and pressure. The load you are carrying now is simply too much for anyone. This is a potential crisis point. However, a sensible assessment of this truth can lead to remedy very quickly. Change must come right now, and you must be prepared to take whatever actions are necessary to recover your balance. The first approach would be to delegate duties and responsibilities to others, who can take some of the load off you. A redistribution of weight will lighten the burden and also create less chance for error arising from the present load. As you are taking on too much, some of it is not being done as well as it could be. Several simple solutions can be found to alter the strains and stresses that are so potentially hazardous now. Find others who can help, and decide your absolute priorities. Putting some smaller tasks aside for a while may not have the disastrous results you fear. Probably, one or more tasks can wait. Be clear, and consult your own conscience. This is like a high-water mark in a flood; it won't remain forever, but it is vital to take action now to ease the build-up. It is very important not to panic, but to be firm and sensible in what you ask of yourself. If you attend to these important truths, all will be well, and good fortune will come from it.

28

The moving lines

If any of your throws produced three identical coins (suns or moons), this is called a moving line. Read the relevant line(s) below, then change the line(s) to the opposite symbol, and look up and read the new forecast (see pages 44–5). Don't forget that your tablet of throws is written from the bottom up, so your first throw is the bottom one.

◗ If your first throw produced all moon coins: be cautious, be ready to spread the load, and take whatever steps are necessary to preserve your own sound health and mind. You are suffering under undue pressures – they are temporary, but no less important for that. Take care to cushion the impact of everything you are required to see to, and lay good foundations for what is ahead. Also, delegate tasks.

● If your second throw produced all sun coins: there may be an unusual or unexpected way to handle the stress you are presently experiencing. If you are very young, turn to someone much older – you will be surprised what a help this proves; if you are someone older, a very young mind can ease your burdens in a way that would amaze you. In extraordinary times, extraordinary measures succeed.

● If your third throw was all sun coins: be very careful now and don't plunge headlong into greater trouble by persisting in a course of overwork. You are carrying too much, and it would be a mistake to imagine you can do this for much longer. Stubborn resistance to good sense will injure you, and others will be unwilling to help you, too, if you don't relent and ask for assistance graciously.

● If your fourth throw brings all sun coins: you will have an offer of help from someone whom you may feel is unable to shoulder the load properly, but even a child can help you adjust the weight you bear now. However, do not abuse this privilege and demand more than you need. Moderation and balance will ensure success for everyone.

● If your fifth throw produces all sun coins: a relationship may be formed with someone who is vastly different from you, but neither misery nor real joy stem from it. Look carefully at the nature of a close tie now, and ask honestly what your expectations are.

◗ If your final throw is all moons: the crisis has now reached its highest point – you may feel engulfed by your troubles. However, the disaster is not as bad as it seems. Allow things to take their course, and even when the worst may happen, the world will not end!

29 The rushing river

This forecast is doubly Water, so has even more impact if you are Water, the second son. This suggests that the period you are entering is one of utmost importance.

To thine own self be true. In this reading, the image of water is deep indeed: water is both above and below, and thus everything is fluid and in motion. Water supports life forms, and also causes intense movement and energy. This outpouring of energy is required, for in your present situation there is much activity, and you need to keep your head to deal with the vigorous rushing of water and movement of the tides. Water can be dangerous if not respected. On the other hand, nothing is stagnant, and movement and change are ahead. So, if this is your reading, it is essential to be like water: to be true to your own feeling nature, and to move on with persistence, watering the drier places, bringing moisture and energy where there has been none. You must think deeply about a situation that demands your full attention, your caution, and your tireless vision. By considering carefully the events around you, and by staying sincere and honest with yourself and others no matter what difficulties seem to surround you, your heart and courage will lead you out of the highest and deepest waters, unerringly. This period will test your capacity to master your own demons; but also your willingness to stay with a situation or set of circumstances no matter how testing they become, no matter how heavy-going the road. If you have heart and courage, and if you stay true to your own ideals and moral instincts, you will not only come through the danger, but will flourish afterwards. Like water flowing ceaselessly, you can not only reach your goal but also find a true sense of destiny and belonging. And, as water describes the soul and feelings, the goal will be partly spiritual.

29

The moving lines

If any of your throws produced three identical coins (suns or moons), this is called a moving line. Read the relevant line(s) below, then change the line(s) to the opposite symbol, and look up and read the new forecast (see pages 44–5). Don't forget that your tablet of throws is written from the bottom up, so your first throw is the bottom one.

◗ If your first throw results in three moon coins: it must not become a habit to take chances and live dangerously to the point of stupidity. Use wisdom to differentiate between dangers that are necessary to endure and those that just provide an adrenalin boost. Be sure to choose between bravery and folly!

● If your second throw produces three sun coins: be wary, for you are entering some very testing situations, and your attention must not wander. The first thing to do is assess the situation without panic, and then take the smallest steps to surmount troubles a little at a time. Do not try to resolve the entire problem in one go, but break the dangers into manageable events. Get through one day at a time, and think of the full picture only as matters improve steadily.

◗ If your third throw brings three moon coins: you still have to tread very carefully, picking your way along a very rough track. Haste will only see you in greater danger, so you must take things as calmly and carefully as possible, one step after another, until a way is gradually found through the mire. Neither doubling back, nor rushing forward in spurts, will bring you to safety. Take your time.

◗ If your fourth throw is all moon coins: don't look to be congratulated for good tasks that you complete now. The most important considerations are about wise moves and a good heart, with a clear head. Count as your reward the successful emergence from a difficult time, not the appreciation of the crowd.

● If your fifth throw produces three sun coins: this is not the moment for huge ambitions. It is most to your advantage to take a conservative estimate of what you must attempt, and leave larger goals for a sunnier day. For now, the important thing to do is simply to escape from the difficulties in which you have found yourself. Do not try to build Rome in a day!

◗ If your sixth and final throw gives you three moon coins: this line suggests an impasse, where there is no straight path emerging from the present circumstances. Good management is required. With a view to correcting a serious past error, there is a necessary period ahead – perhaps as much as three years – during which some recompense and adjustment must be made to make up finally for a previous loss of sight or direction. This is not a cause for misery, but for accepting the necessary remedy for a past mistake. With time, you will come free.

30 Radiance

This forecast is made up of double Fire, so has double the impact if you are the second daughter (Fire). This would indicate you are moving into a peak moment of your life.

Perfect harmony! This reading stands for the radiance of nature: it is through clinging to those dear to you, and to a natural order, that brightness comes. This is a propitious time; it is the best moment to carry out work that requires energy. You are emanating light and warmth to those around you; this partly comes from an inner radiance. You may understand your own worth, value your own feelings, and be fed by a certainty that comes like a spring from within. Success is certain, because you respect the importance of those around you and have proper self-respect as well. Life is dependent upon a series of balanced relationships, even with the sun and the moon and the heavens and the earth. Just as fire requires something to fuel it, you need the nourishment and sustenance you gain in the world. But equally, you give much of yourself to those who need you to light their way, or give them illumination. At present, you have tranquillity of spirit combined with powerful personal energy; the appropriate capacity for both dependence and responsibility. If this were to refer to a relationship, it would point to perfect harmony; if it is to a personal direction or goal, it is to the best balance of patience and forcefulness. To stay on your chosen path is the best course of action. A harmonious way to go about it would be to make use of the ideas and energies of someone or several people, and at the same time to be of use to them. All that comes to you is of your own doing: you have a fire within to accomplish something, and you have a light that guides you even when others feel it is dark. Your role may be to open up spaces that were closed, and to enlighten others as you go. In every case, your brightness will be the vital ingredient.

30

The moving lines

If any of your throws produced three identical coins (suns or moons), this is called a moving line. Read the relevant line(s) below, then change the line(s) to the opposite symbol, and look up and read the new forecast (see pages 44–5). Don't forget that your tablet of throws is written from the bottom up, so your first throw is the bottom one.

● If the first throw resulted in all sun coins: no matter how confusing the path seems to be, a serious focus on what you have to get through in the course of a day will see you through. You are picking your way through a series of confusing options, making sense of a kaleidoscope of images. Your inner calm assures a good outcome.

◖ If your second throw resulted in three moon coins: this is a positive time, like the brightest sun at midday. You have a good mind and have gained an artistic appreciation of the world and of other people; in this positive light, everything appears clear before you. Excellent fortune comes from your quests.

● If your third throw was all sun coins: the test now is of how to deal with a diminishing situation. If an issue or situation or relationship is coming to a gentle conclusion – as at the sunset of a day – it is useless to lament what is gone. Look forward to whatever may be, and prepare your mind and attitude. This is not the moment to lose your head or bemoan changes that must come; it is time to adjust to new opportunities.

● If your fourth throw produces all sun coins: it is of the utmost importance to pace yourself now, and not to create a meteoric flash of light which quickly fades, like fireworks in the sky. Life is a distance race, requiring staying power. Do not become inflamed or expend your vital energy needlessly; you will waste yourself on something which is ultimately not important for your life as a whole.

◗ If your fifth throw produced three moon coins: from past and present pain, total clarity of mind is earned. Thus you have the awareness to turn grief into joy, the joy becoming more radiant because of the pang of grief. The future turns out well from this philosophical way of viewing the world, and from your clear and purposeful thoughts.

● If your final throw resulted in all sun coins: don't be too hard on yourself, or critical of others. It is important to drop some bad habits you have acquired, or are on the verge of allowing to become routine; but if you ask too much of yourself, or of someone close to you, you may risk a complete failure of relationship or goal. This is a time to weed out the worst offences, but to be tolerant too. Success has a better chance if you are realistic rather than obsessive.

31 Romance blossoms

This forecast is composed of Mountain and Lake, so has even greater importance for a third or subsequent son (Mountain) or daughter (Lake). In either case, this would suggest you are entering into a period of peak importance.

Exceptional good fortune! The powers of attraction between the sexes are pictured in this delightful balance between male and female, sun and moon. There is unity between the more vulnerable and the stronger aspects of us all, individually and in partnership. There is perfect harmony between stillness and joy, poise and motion. Just as a mountain is doubled and extended by being reflected in a lake, creating beauty, so this reading tells us of a relationship between two people which is beautiful, harmonious, and has the power to unite the two in a graceful blend. The lake is fed by the mountain's melting streams; the mountain finds its natural rest in the lake that mirrors its image and extends its impact. A man and woman joined together in this same way are in complete accord. If this is your reading, you will succeed in any enterprise you undertake, whether or not it concerns love and relationships. But it's important to persevere, not to shrink back and give up. A courtship between an attracted couple needs persistence from at least one of them: the wooing that feeds the spark and sees a relationship blossom from mere attraction to full romance. Here, the female element is stronger, gaining respect and precedence in the pairing (at least temporarily), as the lake is on top of the mountain. Thus, your best strategy may be to go after something you wish for deeply, even if you feel you are asking for something greater than you. Success comes from joyful boldness; and yet everything is in proportion, with no excess. Free your mind and open to exceptional possibilities: the extraordinary may well be possible!

31

The moving lines

If any of your throws produced three identical coins (suns or moons), this is called a moving line. Read the relevant line(s) below, then change the line(s) to the opposite symbol, and look up and read the new forecast (see pages 44–5). Don't forget that your tablet of throws is written from the bottom up, so your first throw is the bottom one.

◗ If your first throw resulted in all moon coins: change and motion – going after something dear to you – are apparent. You are already aware, in the smallest way, of the need to shift. However, as yet, no one knows what you have in mind, so no one counters your intentions.

◗ If your second throw presented all moon coins: there is a moment of uncertainty, and you are caught between motion and stillness – between going after an important goal or dream, and being frozen with doubt or fear. Wait just as long as you need in order to dispel your hesitations. If your idea is sound, you will soon feel impelled to act. Until this certainty arrives, your plans are only half formed, and your energies only half committed.

● If your third throw resulted in all sun coins: your heart dictates an action that may be premature. Don't run after someone you wish to be of importance to, but be ready to hold back a little. Neither should you allow someone to dictate an action to you that feels wrong. It may be perfectly fair and wise to desist, at the moment, from any course of action you feel inhibited by.

● If your fourth throw was all sun coins: persevere now! The way is clear for you to act, so act with commitment. All doubts evaporate, and sadness about the past is no longer a reason to inhibit your future happiness and direction. Your prime concern should not be to influence others to follow you, but to act with the sincerity of your own heart. Good fortune comes from pure intentions.

● If your fifth throw is all sun coins: your feelings come instinctively, and in this instance they are married to a firm will. You cannot cross-examine these instinctive reactions, but must respect them.

◗ If your sixth and final throw is all moon coins: actions speak louder than words, but here, it may be that someone is trying to talk you into a position. This is unlikely to move you! Equally, if you are merely trying to influence someone through speech, you will be lacking real power to convince. In this situation, words are not enough.

32 A strong marriage

This forecast is made up of Wind and Thunder, so has greater impact if you are either the eldest daughter (Wind), or the eldest son (Thunder). As such, you are entering a key moment of life-changing significance.

Be steadfast, yet ever flexible! Thunder and wind go together in nature; the two work well in unison. Both elements are individually powerful, but they blend together to influence the climate and change the state of affairs. Together, they will bring a storm, which can refresh or damage the world around it. In this case, this image is of endurance: two strong elements in balance, unhindered by other obstacles, blended to powerful effect. Like a lasting marriage, there is no state of rest between the two entities, but a constantly renewing source of energy, or cyclical moods and emotions, which has the power to endure over time. This reading tells us that constant energy can have a lasting effect; it is suggestive of a need to move, to make a trip, to set out on a venture. It's not a moment to be idle. The wind symbolizes an outward breath – either gentle or powerful – which is felt by others. Thunder, likewise, is heard for miles. The rolling thunder and blowing wind are always shifting, changing, moving; but they are also constant in the certainty of their return. Stand firmly now for what you want to achieve, be true to your decisions, and be ready to act. Your chosen direction is good, but you must be flexible about any changes that may be required. The destination should stand, but the route you take may need to be altered. You must be able to adjust without losing your overall path; a strong, long-married couple learn to acclimatize to new situations and demands, their adaptability ensuring their continuing unity. Persevere, for success awaits you.

32

The moving lines

If any of your throws produced three identical coins (suns or moons), this is called a moving line. Read the relevant line(s) below, then change the line(s) to the opposite symbol, and look up and read the new forecast (see pages 44–5). Don't forget that your tablet of throws is written from the bottom up, so your first throw is the bottom one.

◗ If your first throw produced all moon coins: don't seek too much too soon. Hastiness will produce poor results, so allow matters to develop properly.

● If your second throw produced all sun coins: under no circumstances should you feel responsible or remorseful about the way a situation has developed. Control of your own feelings and inner motivations is all you can answer for, and doing so will not inflame the situation even further. Be responsible for yourself alone.

● If your third throw produced all sun coins: you must avoid being buffeted by outside opinion, or allowing your mood to be affected by others. Again, you must be your own best counsel, and dismiss the prattle of others.

● If your fourth throw brought all sun coins: you may be looking in the wrong place for what you seek. In this case, no amount of waiting will help. Be ready to alter the details of your original plans, and look for the desired overall results by other means.

◗ If your fifth throw brought all moon coins: there are times when it is right to adhere to customs and manners, or to the tradition of the times; but this is not the case now. Your current circumstances may require a new approach to a problem, and you must be flexible enough to cope with this. Things do not remain the same forever, and you must be guided by the needs of the present hour.

◗ If your sixth and final throw produced all moon coins: restlessness is natural sometimes, but at the moment it is a threat to accomplishing your desired state of affairs. Inner composure is demanded, as well as the sense to remain focused while there are jobs to be done.

33 Keep it simple

This forecast, made up of Mountain and Sky, will have even greater impact for you if you are either the third or younger son (Mountain) or a father (Sky). In either case this indicates you are entering a key moment in your life.

Success comes from small projects. This reading relates, time-wise, to the period just after the peak of summer when the light and the days are drawing in. This is not the moment to start on big adventures or major projects. During the darker winter months, a different pattern of life emerges; it is beneficial to look at life in a more precise and focused way, rather than with an expansive view. This is a good time to draw in your horns and attend to small tasks that can be performed quietly: to do a bit of DIY rather than building a new home. In this reading, the darker days are seen as a corollary of difficulty, so at this time it would be wise to tighten your boundaries: metaphorically to come indoors for protection, rather than stay out in the long summer evenings. Just as it would not be sensible to go for a walk during an electrical thunderstorm, neither is this the best time to embark on a major new project. Success comes now from working on several small tasks that are not necessarily designed to make a big impact in the future. If you have large scale, life-changing plans in mind, consider the present climate as unhelpful. This will not always be so, but for the moment, outside forces are not with you. Put simply, it is not a time to go into battle, nor a time to be drawn into a fight. It is a time to withdraw – even to be temporarily unavailable – while other influences are allowed to unfold and play a part that will become more evident later. Retreating, then, is not a sign of weakness or cowardice at this time: it is a sign of wisdom and perceptiveness.

33

The moving lines

If any of your throws produced three identical coins (suns or moons), this is called a moving line. Read the relevant line(s) below, then change the line(s) to the opposite symbol, and look up and read the new forecast (see pages 44–5). Don't forget that your tablet of throws is written from the bottom up, so your first throw is the bottom one.

◗ If your first throw produces all moon coins: this is a very significant moment – a time when you are most 'exposed' to risk. The best option is to keep very still and quiet.

◗ If your second throw is all moon coins: holding very tightly to a railing can prevent a fall on even the most dangerous stairs. So it is now: hold fast to something tangible that guides your steps. This might be the advice of someone you look up to, or respect. Adhering to what gives you strength in times of stress will pull you through a testing time.

● If your third throw is all sun coins: you may feel you have no freedom of action now – little choice of movement or direction. But there is some comfort to be found in one or two people near at hand who will not desert you in your hour of vulnerability. Good fortune comes from recognizing these loyal souls.

● If your fourth throw is all sun coins: you assess the situation rightly, and understand that drawing back is the best way to cope with adverse circumstances. Good fortune and success come to you from this awareness, and those standing against you will lose their hold sooner or later.

● If your fifth throw produces all sun coins: a friendly disengagement from dispute is available to you now, and this is the correct course to take. It is in your best interests – and certain to bring a good result ultimately – if you recognize this as the right moment to make a good-natured retreat from any conflict.

● If your final throw results in three sun coins: your mood is hopeful and positive as you see the way clear to bringing an end to a quarrel or confrontation without any loss of face or self-esteem. Your mood is right, and good will certainly come from this gesture. You are free to leave on your own terms.

34 Wise judgement

As it is made up of Sky and Thunder, this reading has more impact still if you are either Sky, a father, and/or Thunder, an eldest son. In both cases this would suggest a key moment in your life is just ahead.

This reading is very positive. It indicates that you have now achieved a perfect blend of strength and understanding at a very opportune moment; this can have a life-changing effect. To undertake any challenge, especially when the road ahead is largely unknown, takes good preparation as well as strength of character and will. Ultimately we can account for no one's behaviour but our own; but it is to your own moral strength that you now must turn. You may have come to a deep realization about what will be just and fair to you and to others concerned with you. Such conscience and good sense helps you to forge ahead with a plan of action that will make you happy and bring you closer to your desired goals for your whole life. What is also important is that you find a way to do this without trampling on someone else's happiness and self-esteem. You may have found yourself in better harmony with those closest to you than ever before; or you may have discovered a way of living well and in tune with your own sense of ethics, which at the same time brings many positive aspects to your social life. Your energy and physical determination are at a peak, and you have the staying power to accomplish any ambition. Good fortune is deserved, and you will feel both vibrant and at peace at the same time: a wonderful balance. Any status you achieve now will not be hollow, but will have been well earned. This is a rosy time and, if your choices are good and wise, your whole life's future direction will benefit. This forecast is also strongly concerned with the last month of winter, when its full effect will be felt.

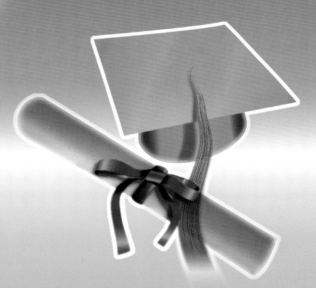

34

The moving lines

If any of your throws produced three identical coins (suns or moons), this is called a moving line. Read the relevant line(s) below, then change the line(s) to the opposite symbol, and look up and read the new forecast (see pages 44–5). Don't forget that your tablet of throws is written from the bottom up, so your first throw is the bottom one.

● If your first throw is all sun coins: more thought is required at this point, to decide how best to actualize a goal you have set yourself. At present, the energy for movement is only in your toes: it must generate more power yet, before actual advance is warranted. Think on!

● If your second throw is all sun coins: obstacles recede now, and opportunities develop more clearly. With real persistence, and the willingness to work on a good plan of attack, the door to success begins to open for you.

● If your third throw produces all sun coins: if you are tempted to sing your own praises too loudly – even though the job is well done – you will meet with resistance and disapproval rather than admiration. Be sure it is the satisfaction of a difficult job well discharged that drives you, rather than the expectation of gratitude from others, or the idea that you will impress someone you would like to influence. Some modesty is demanded here.

● If your fourth throw results in all sun coins: the way to achieve your goal now is to work quietly towards a removal of those things that stand in your way; this you can do diligently, and without hurting anyone else. Continual gentle persuasion, little gestures that combine to become greater ones, will accomplish the end you desire.

◗ If your fifth throw has produced all moon coins: there is no longer any need to lock horns with an adversary, even in the most tactful way. Problems seem to resolve themselves, and hurdles disappear. Stubbornness is not required now, just a relaxed approach to everyone and everything.

◗ If your last throw has produced all moon coins: don't allow egotism to drive you too far forward now. With your goal accomplished, don't think of taking matters further than sensibly required. This last throw is concerned with mastering the ego and acting with balance. Trouble comes from excess of any kind.

35 A beautiful sunrise

This reading is made up of Earth and Fire, and therefore has greater significance if you are either a mother (Earth), and/or a second daughter (Fire). In this case a key moment is suggested, which will have impact for some time to come.

Success through perfect harmony and balance. In this forecast the sun is seen rising beautifully over the earth – the beginning of a perfect sunny day. The whole image signifies progress and creative harmony. Someone with power and influence, who is also humane and sensible, may understand the wisdom of working hand in hand with another person of clarity and intelligence. Even if one person is perceived as being of a higher status, it is the co-operation between two great minds working towards a mutually advantageous result that is important. Moreover, many other people will benefit from this union. If this is your reading, you may be one or other of these two people. You may be the self-sufficient person of intelligence and ability who sees how desirable it is to work with another like-minded soul, even if they seem to be socially or economically 'above' you. Or, you could be the more highly regarded individual who nevertheless does not suffer from arrogance, and understands what this other talented person can offer. In either case, co-operation is desirable, and will have lasting positive effects for many people. Together with a partner whom you should be able to recognize easily, you can create a newer world, and a brighter day. Jealousy is not an issue for either of you; like the bright sun, you have risen above the ordinary world. Now, it is the uniting of talent, and the marriage of two distinctive and highly regarded people, that brings happiness and success to many. Further, your sense of joy and satisfaction from the joining of these two forces is assured. Something truly significant is developing, and a golden age is dawning.

35

The moving lines

If any of your throws produced three identical coins (suns or moons), this is called a moving line. Read the relevant line(s) below, then change the line(s) to the opposite symbol, and look up and read the new forecast (see pages 44–5). Don't forget that your tablet of throws is written from the bottom up, so your first throw is the bottom one.

◗ If your first throw is three moon coins: you need to carry on now with something you know to be right. Even if you find that others you must deal with don't understand your ideas, you can still persevere with your aims and, in time, you may be sure that good will come from them.

◗ When your second throw is all moon coins: there is an issue you must deal with before you can move forward towards your goal. You may even meet with outright opposition. But even in difficulty, the only option is to continue, with as much gentleness and diplomacy as you can muster.

◗ If your third throw gives three moon coins: other people will now be free to come to your aid. There is a mutual understanding between various parties about what will work for everyone.

● If your fourth throw results in three sun coins: make sure that whatever work or actions you commit to now are worthy of being seen and understood by others. If you feel the need to work in the dark – without openness – problems will arise.

◗ If your fifth throw produces all moon coins: it is important not to put too much emphasis on winning or losing now. Just do the job in hand to the best of your ability, and everything will turn out well. If your motives are just for fame and fortune, this will not result in success.

● If your final throw is all sun coins: you need to be on the offensive now, and commit a great deal of energy and positive aggression to the situation. But you also need to be aware that this initiative might make you some enemies and perhaps cause you some personal regrets.

36 The darkening day

This reading is a combination of Fire and Earth, so it has even greater impact if you are a second daughter (Fire) and/or a mother (Earth). In this case this time will be of special significance in your life.

Success comes through great caution. It is important to recognize that this reading is not a forecast of problems to come; rather, it depicts a moment for extreme care in relation to other people. How you handle your situation now is vital. It may be the most lonely of times in one sense, for no one else's advice is going to help: you must be your own best advisor, and go it alone if possible. Indeed, contact from anyone else – especially someone who looks to be a leader or advisor – is likely to cause you to lose your way. The most important thing to do now is to resist pressure from someone else. Being swept along under a bad regime is no excuse for acting foolishly; but to resist a person who has some influence over you is never easy. The way to achieve this, perhaps, is to be outwardly calm, while inwardly remaining true to good principles which can guide you through. The darkening day is a metaphor for the disappearance of light. This means both lack of advice, and of goodness. Nothing now can be taken at face value – it is harder to see in the dark. Only your subtlest intuition can guide you, and every step must be taken carefully. But, with good sense and by keeping your wits about you, you can overcome your difficulties. You must keep some personal qualities to yourself; you will know which these are. It may be necessary to remain private, even secret, in order to stay calm under provocation. A clear way through a tangled situation can only be found by refusing to give in to anybody unscrupulous; and by staying calm and strong in your own beliefs. At first this is a necessity for survival – ultimately, it leads to triumph and good fortune.

36

The moving lines

If any of your throws produced three identical coins (suns or moons), this is called a moving line. Read the relevant line(s) below, then change the line(s) to the opposite symbol, and look up and read the new forecast (see pages 44–5). Don't forget that your tablet of throws is written from the bottom up, so your first throw is the bottom one.

● If your first throw produces all sun coins: you are faced with a test of character and integrity. As the light of the day is fading, this is not the moment to take off into the darkness. The climate is not apt for venturing out, as you cannot see clearly what is ahead. Try to stay true to yourself, even if other people misunderstand your intentions, or worse, misreport you. Your own strength is enough.

◗ If your second throw produces all moon coins: any insults you receive from a lower-minded person won't be fatal. Most importantly, concern yourself with trying to avoid hurt to others, more than to yourself. This noble aim is in your favour, and fortune comes to you in a dark moment.

● If your third throw produces all sun coins: you are in a position to gain the upper hand over someone who has been harassing you. Chance – fate – takes a hand in events, to your favour; but it will still be some time before events settle down and a clear way forward is found.

◗ If your fourth throw produces all moon coins: pushing against a brick wall will not produce results now. Information may come to you, showing you the thoughts and intended actions of someone acting against your wishes; but all you can do with this information is to take a step back for now. Staying close will only result in you being in the middle of the storm when it breaks.

◗ If your fifth throw brings three moon coins: this is truly a stressful moment, but you are equal to it. Don't lose your way by giving in to the inclinations of someone who wants you to compromise yourself. No matter how difficult, be sure your actions satisfy your own conscience.

◗ If your final throw produces all moon coins: just at the moment when it seems as though a tyrant will succeed and get things their own way, they lose their power and vanish without trace. Even in the face of the worst despair, don't give up your inner sunshine, for it is this that will help you through the difficulties that seem to have surrounded you. The mists will soon clear, if you do not lose hope.

37 Women united

Being made up of Fire and Wind, this reading has even greater personal significance if you are either a second daughter (Fire), or the eldest daughter (Wind). In both cases this would suggest that a defining moment in your life is unfolding now.

Success comes from the strength of women. This reading celebrates the endurance of women within the family – the powerful ability of the females to put their personal wishes aside in favour of nurturing other members of their household. In this instance, the two sisters are in the foreground and, working together, they spread greater light and warmth. The wind, acting like bellows, fans the flames; and the fire itself can create a wind of its own – the draught that spreads warmth and burns evenly, sustaining life. So it is that women working together for a unified cause will achieve their end. The forecast suggests the desirability of working with another female in your family – or perhaps a sisterly character in your life who fills that role – in order to overcome any present difficulties and reach a goal to which you both aspire. Along the way the family benefits as a whole, and others who are linked with you also prosper as a family. Everything can be attained now through co-operation. There should be no jealousy, and no rivalry, merely a close psychological understanding of everyone concerned. Loyalty will have its natural reward; mutual affection guarantees the smooth running of affairs and gentle progress towards a dream. The other vital ingredient for success is the marriage of actions with words – words alone cannot achieve a cherished goal. If you balance deeds, affections and loyalty in harmony, pursuing the same course of action, then all will be well and very good fortune will come to you.

37

The moving lines

If any of your throws produced three identical coins (suns or moons), this is called a moving line. Read the relevant line(s) below, then change the line(s) to the opposite symbol, and look up and read the new forecast (see pages 44–5). Don't forget that your tablet of throws is written from the bottom up, so your first throw is the bottom one.

● If your first throw is three sun coins: from the beginning of any project you should concentrate on the delegation and careful briefing of individual tasks. You will be very successful in what you set out to achieve if each person understands his or her role from the outset.

◗ If your second throw produces all moon coins: despite an apparently restricted role, the mother of the house exerts the most influence. Consider your position and look at how you can have a far-reaching impact. Be prepared to find an alternative to forceful behaviour, or aggression, to achieve the influence you wish for; by concentrating on the work in hand, a greater power than is first apparent is yours.

● If your third throw is all sun coins: strive for a balance between discipline and laughter now. It is vital to keep your humour in times of conflict and not to ruin good relationships with bad-tempered stubbornness. However, some firmness and expression of disapproval may be not only acceptable but essential. Mutual respect must be established.

If your fourth throw produces three moon coins: happiness comes now from finding a good balance between work and leisure, laughter and seriousness, income and expenditure. It is crucial to ensure that your life is in harmonious balance: you must live within your means physically, emotionally and materially. Success is guaranteed as you find good advice, and follow it.

If your fifth throw produces all sun coins: someone who exercises control or influence over you is nevertheless not someone to fear or doubt. You are in good hands.

If your final throw produces three sun coins: you must ensure that what you do with your life commands respect from others, and also accords you a huge degree of self-respect. If you are not at ease with the role you play in your working life, unhappiness will result. If, however, you can accept your responsibilities and be happy with the path you follow, only good fortune can come of it. It is important, therefore, to attend to the direction of your life.

38 Contradiction

A combination of Lake and Fire, this reading has even more significance if you are the third or younger daughter (Lake), or the second daughter (Fire). In either case this indicates a moment of key importance ahead.

Success comes through close attention to detail. There appears to be a lack of agreement now between two strong-willed women. Any attempts to achieve a unity of purpose are proving difficult, since both are strong characters and see things very differently. However, if an open state of conflict can be avoided, and a gentle agreement to disagree is allowed to prevail, then some good can come from this situation. The best way to avoid real trouble is to take care of a myriad of small details, which in any case need your attention. Neither one person nor the other can get their own way entirely, and at the moment compromise seems unlikely. But not all opposition between people is a bad thing, as two different viewpoints can give rise to new creative opportunities. New approaches and understandings are born from contradictions. Your best option now is to take great care and put great effort into individual tasks. Smaller ventures that don't cause such clashes, or demand big decisions, can be very successfully undertaken, with very good results. In fact, it can be both justified and positive for two strong people to maintain their individuality, not to give in to a view so strongly opposed to his or her own. The test is to remember that individuality and a different point of view can be maintained without enmity, and to recognize that differences don't have to lead to isolation. Perhaps there is no absolute right or wrong, and both views can be allowed. Working together on one big project won't be possible, so tackle small individual jobs. Maintain your sense of humour even during this disagreement between two otherwise closely related people.

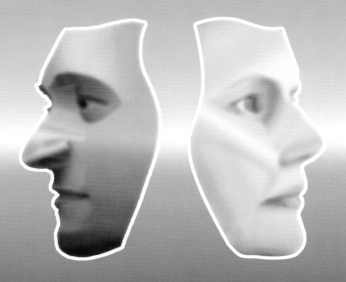

38

The moving lines

If any of your throws produced three identical coins (suns or moons), this is called a moving line. Read the relevant line(s) below, then change the line(s) to the opposite symbol, and look up and read the new forecast (see pages 44–5). Don't forget that your tablet of throws is written from the bottom up, so your first throw is the bottom one.

● If your first throw resulted in three sun coins: don't try to subdue a different opinion from your own by force of will. If someone's views are contrary to yours, let that be: to harass them would be undignified. Either allow them to come back through their own choice, aware that a misunderstanding has occurred, or let them go, their lives to take another course. Good fortune will arise from this flexibility of character.

● If your second throw produced three sun coins: an issue may have unfolded that makes it difficult for two people who are usually close to get together. Try to arrange an informal meeting in a neutral place, or an accidental get-together. If there is any true feeling between them, this will help to set things right again.

◗ If your third throw resulted in three moon coins: don't despair if everything seems to be going against you, or threatening you. Your good temper and cheerfulness may be tested to the limit, but all will come out well if you remain loyal to those whom you love, and who love you.

● If your fourth throw resulted in three sun coins: although you may have been feeling cut off and at odds with everyone around you, a like-minded person will now come into your life with whom you can find some peace and equilibrium. Much can be accomplished with this new relationship.

◗ If your fifth throw produced all moon coins: it is sometimes hard to know whether a new acquaintance is sincere or not – a potential friend or someone who is indifferent to you. But soon, someone about whom you have been undecided shows their true colours, and you will realize you have an ally. Together you can work towards a positive aim.

● If your final throw resulted in three sun coins: you have isolated yourself from someone who would naturally help you. But eventually you understand their best intentions, and can dismiss your doubts and watchfulness. There is real delight in this reunion of two suited friends, and tensions will dissolve. From a position of apparent opposition, closeness is the lasting legacy.

39 Hindrance

This forecast is made up of Mountain and Water, so has even greater significance if you are either a third or younger son (Mountain), or a second son (Water). In both cases this suggests a moment of peak importance about to unfold.

Success comes through steadiness and focus. The image of this reading is about being caught between an impenetrable mountain and a dangerous body of water: caution is demanded. There are obstacles all around you, but going at them full on will not clear them. It's essential to pause and assess the degree of danger. In fact, it would be better to stop entirely until you have given everything much thought. But a decision to retreat from danger doesn't mean you are running away. Rather, you are considering events from a necessary position of objectivity, from which you will prepare to overcome your difficulties. There is someone wise, who commands your respect, to whom it would be helpful to go now for what will be excellent advice and judgement. You are facing a dilemma that is almost impossible to see through by yourself. By joining forces with someone calm and sensible you will be less likely to respond in an irrational way to the issues. Perseverance will almost certainly be part of the solution. Unwavering focus will ensure your good fortune, but it is not in your interest to try to force a path through the mire. Your present difficulties won't last; it's how you approach them that will be of defining, and lasting, significance. Along the way, you will learn something very important about yourself and about the desirability of working with a well-chosen partner or partners. Turn your attentions inward, ponder anything within your own position that could be adjusted to see things more clearly. It would be useless to become angry about your predicament, but wholly desirable to become more flexible in your approach to it.

39

The moving lines

If any of your throws produced three identical coins (suns or moons), this is called a moving line. Read the relevant line(s) below, then change the line(s) to the opposite symbol, and look up and read the new forecast (see pages 44–5). Don't forget that your tablet of throws is written from the bottom up, so your first throw is the bottom one.

◗ If the first throw produced all moon coins: it is definitely in your interest to pull back from any confrontation now. Retreating for the time being will lead to improved circumstances in the future, whereas pushing against the grain will cause greater problems.

◗ If your second throw produced three moon coins: you are facing a difficult encounter, and it would be better to back off. However, in this particular situation, you may have no choice but to push forward and encounter the struggle, as you are duty-bound to do so. You may not meet with success, or make the obstacles melt away, but you must see things through and exhaust all possible avenues of discussion.

● If your third throw produced three sun coins: to pursue your goal at the moment will definitely bring you into serious difficulty, and any efforts would be reckless. The only way to cope at present is to stand back and think again. If you push on, you will fail.

◗ If your fourth throw brought three moon coins: on your own, you cannot now manage the trials before you. You need support, and you must also be prepared to take a longer way around in order to succeed. Be ready to take a step back and find a different approach to your problem.

● If your fifth throw resulted in three sun coins: although you may feel completely hemmed in and unable to see a way forward, in the most worrying moment friends will appear and offer tremendous help. You may feel you are almost reaching a crisis point, but don't panic. A way out of trouble will come with a co-operative ally who will not let you down.

◗ If your final throw resulted in three moon coins: this is truly the moment to ask for help. Someone you respect will be there if you need them, and only by consulting with a person of such power and education or position will you find a route through what seems like an impassable road. All will be well.

40 Resolution

This forecast is made up of Water and Thunder, so the reading has an even greater impact if you are either a second son (Water), or an eldest son (Thunder). This would indicate that a period of key importance is unfolding.

Success! A way through difficulties is found. This reading is connected with the preceding one, 39 Hindrance. It is the next phase, when a way out of difficulty has started to emerge. All the tensions and frustrations of a difficult period are melting away rapidly; if not yet entirely: there is a feeling of the load lightening and a way being found through the darkest times. Suddenly, the relief will become clear, and hope surges again. A trip will now contribute to an improvement in all conditions, but it may also add an element of joy. This moment of change has lasting and profound impact, for the future will be substantially altered. This is partly because of the deeper understanding you come to after a release from pressure – a greater appreciation of your own inner strength and capacity to weather difficult storms. It is also due to a sense of relief that the worst is over, and a way forward has been found not merely to survival, but to happiness. Don't be exultant too prematurely, however. There is a way to go, and work to be done, before full freedom comes. Don't try to rush it; push ahead steadily and try to keep to an organized routine. This final period is like the last few days before exams, after a long struggle and the pressure that comes with study. Most of the burden is lifting, but some aspects of the work to complete remain, and there is no way to hurry these final stages. Good fortune will come, indeed, but the last phases of work must be carried out steadily. There may still be some last actions that are necessary to take; be careful to leave nothing unfinished, and no strings untied.

40

The moving lines

If any of your throws produced three identical coins (suns or moons), this is called a moving line. Read the relevant line(s) below, then change the line(s) to the opposite symbol, and look up and read the new forecast (see pages 44–5). Don't forget that your tablet of throws is written from the bottom up, so your first throw is the bottom one.

○ If your first throw produced three moon coins: it is in your interest to proceed without too many words. Talking would be a waste of time. You can see peace ahead of you, freedom from your recent burdens; but it would definitely pay to stay in the background for some time yet.

● If your second throw resulted in three sun coins: wise moves help you to overcome three adversaries who are causing you difficulty with another party – perhaps through their use of flattery or manipulation. The important thing seems to be that you perceive their danger and recognize a clean way of nullifying their power. This line suggests defeat for any party who is working against you in a dishonest way. Straight dealing on your own part is the best plan.

○ If your third throw resulted in three moon coins: it would be wise to play a low-key role here for a while. A narrow escape from troubles, and the end of past woes does not call for arrogant boasting. Keep a low profile, and you will attract no jealousy to you. Everything in moderation would be your best advice for the foreseeable future.

● If your fourth throw produced three sun coins: watch the company you keep now. Many will judge you, and your companions will have an impact on your future happiness. You are yourself noble and gracious: keep like-minded friends!

◗ If your fifth throw produced three moon coins: the separation between you and someone else is very desirable – and you will know why. But you will not be able to break free if you are not truly determined to do so. Only when your mind is absolutely resolved to let go will the other party give up and truly release you.

◗ If your final throw produced three moon coins: you must finally become disentangled from someone who is leeching your strength and wearing you down. Only radical means will free you, and there is no half-way measure. If you cannot accomplish this, you are bound to experience true pain for some time yet. Making up your mind is the first step; but it must be followed by serious action. Ongoing suffering must be put to an end now.

41 Imbalance

This forecast is composed of Lake and Mountain, so has even greater impact for you if you are either the third or younger daughter (Lake), or son (Mountain). This would suggest a moment of peak importance is occurring.

Success comes through restraint. This reading indicates a decrease in material riches. This is not a forecast of doom or despair, but it suggests you should recognize that this is a moment to be pragmatic about what is available to you, and that you should trim your sails accordingly. This is particularly relevant in so far as it affects what you wish to project to others; it may be occurring at a time when you feel a need to give off an aura of wealth or material success. The forecast suggests that there is no shame, and no loss of face or confidence, in having to assume simplicity at this time. The simple life – simple dress, simple manners, simple hospitality – is no reason for embarrassment, even when you might like to feel able to be more lavish. It is far more important to consider wisely what restraints are necessary at a time of shortage, and to work within those restraints. At a time of debt, you must address the difficulty and find sensible ways to deal with it. This forecast tells us that restraint is positive, and that nothing important will suffer from this act of trimming away any usual surplus. As long as you act with sincerity and simplicity, all will turn out extremely well. Indeed, the paradox of this reading is that it predicts truly good fortune stemming from the actions you take now. Generous instincts need to be curbed for the time being; but anger at the prevailing circumstances must be avoided. Anger has no place now, and any reasonable success will only be achieved by controlling our feelings. During this time of out-of-the-ordinary life patterns, an unusual clarity of mind is reached. The soul seems to become even more enriched, and wiser.

41

The moving lines

If any of your throws produced three identical coins (suns or moons), this is called a moving line. Read the relevant line(s) below, then change the line(s) to the opposite symbol, and look up and read the new forecast (see pages 44–5). Don't forget that your tablet of throws is written from the bottom up, so your first throw is the bottom one.

● If your first throw produced three sun coins: this concerns the act both of offering help to another person, and of accepting it. If you have time to spare, and it would be helpful to give someone advice or practical assistance, then help should be offered freely. But it is also important, if you are the recipient of help, not to abuse the privilege; too much reliance may cause real ill feeling later.

● If your second throw produced three sun coins: very similarly to the previous throw, this suggests that it is not in the interests of either of two parties ultimately if you exhaust yourself trying to do something for someone else. Be helpful, by all means, but in proportion, and not to your detriment.

◗ If your third throw resulted in three moon coins: there is a strong probability of problems arising now if three people are involved in a journey or project. If all three start off together, only two will finish; but if one starts alone, another friend will join in. Choose your associates wisely now!

If your fourth throw resulted in three moon coins: take great care now about pressures that are coming from others. If you are being asked to act in a way you know to be wrong, many troubles that you cannot begin to see nowwill result if you do so. On the other hand, your refusal to join in with this will soon bring you friends in very high places.

If your fifth throw resulted in three moon coins: this is a lucky throw! Your good fortune is assured now: rewards may even come from more than one direction, and nothing can tarnish your good luck.

If your final throw produced three sun coins: again, luck and rewards are coming to you now, but you are especially blessed, since the good fortune you receive is connected with works that have been beneficial to others. Your efforts have been unselfish, and bring you and others much joy.

42 Setting an example

This forecast, made up of Thunder and Wind, has greater significance for you if you are either an eldest son (Thunder) or an eldest daughter (Wind). Either suggests you are approaching a time of optimum importance.

Self-sacrifice for the common good of others brings success. This forecast concerns the sacrifice of individual desires or momentary wishes for the good of someone younger, or even the generosity of someone powerful, who is prepared to sacrifice his or her own ambitions for the good of those below him/her. A boss, for example, who willingly reduces his own income in order to plough resources back into the company and the wellbeing of the other workers, has the general good of the business at heart – selflessly at this time. Such good spirit and wise understanding is highly beneficial for the general good of everyone. Another view might be someone in charge who is prepared to work even harder than those he or she employs, or muck in and do even the most basic tasks. Everyone pulling together, without arrogance or airs, is the sure foundation of a positive working environment and success in the future. Structured in this way, no business or undertaking can fail. There is no ego and no selfish inclination to impede the real flowering of a positive venture. Everything blossoms: relationships, material benefits, as well as security of position. The image is of Wind and Thunder increasing each other, and bringing together elements that are good for the earth and the climate, recharging and refreshing. The Wind strengthens the Thunder, and the Thunder seems to increase the Wind; the mutual benefits of this exchange are so great that you are encouraged to imitate it. Helping others, you help yourself. Everyone grows in personal esteem from the mutual efforts involved.

42

The moving lines

If any of your throws produced three identical coins (suns or moons), this is called a moving line. Read the relevant line(s) below, then change the line(s) to the opposite symbol, and look up and read the new forecast (see pages 44–5). Don't forget that your tablet of throws is written from the bottom up, so your first throw is the bottom one.

● If your first throw produced three sun coins: exceptional help comes to you from someone in a position of influence, and it would be wise to use it well. You have an opportunity to accomplish some extraordinary achievement now – it's vital to take up this offer and work hard to make it count!

◗ If your second throw resulted in three moon coins: you have been favoured by all the best elements, and luck may now be showered upon you – but it is no more than you deserve for good work and your good relationship with others. Don't allow this unexpected good fortune to make you behave rashly: think carefully how best to employ the wonderful benefits you are experiencing – to your own and others' advantage.

◗ If your third throw produced three moon coins: you are likely to benefit from someone else's misfortune, but it is through no fault of your own. Accept what comes to you with sensitivity and goodness, and all will be well for the future.

If your fourth throw produced three moon coins: your role for the time being may as a go-between, finding a path of agreement between two people. Important consequences will emerge as a result of your advice and diplomacy, but even someone powerful who has a reputation for stern behaviour will listen to you if you speak the truth and act according to your conscience.

If your fifth throw resulted in three sun coins: if your heart and intentions are good, and you know in your soul what is right, good fortune will come to you in what you are trying to accomplish. What you do, you do from kindness, without expecting others to notice and be impressed. Your future looks radiant.

If your final throw produced three sun coins: this suggests that sacrifice for no good end is a waste of energy and wisdom, and may even have unfortunate effects in the future. To act wisely now, sit quietly and think what will ensue from the course you have decided on. How you speak to other people is of profound importance now: rash words will come back to haunt you. Think, before speaking at all!

43 Bursting point!

Made up of Sky and Lake, this reading has even greater significance if you are a father (Sky), or the third or younger daughter (Lake). You are at a key moment in your life.

Success will come through trusting that the future will improve. In the image of this forecast, the water in the lake has reached bursting point and any further rainfall would cause a potential calamity. So it is with human emotions, when passions have reached a point where reasonable thought and behaviour is obscured. Circumstances suggest that, emotionally, a kind of flood point has been reached. This overwrought strength of feeling has the power to annihilate your good sense and cause chaos. One rash act of outpouring emotions may have a devastating impact on the future. Here, you need to find an appropriate way to confront the moment when tempers, or frustrations, or real emotional pain, have come to a point of no return, and something has got to give. The way forward is definitely not to fight, however, for this only puts greater strain on a stressful set of conditions. As difficult as it may be to do so, you must trust that the influence of those people who have caused you harm is on the wain. Conditions are about to change, and a breakthrough will come. Personal passion must be momentarily set aside, and reasonable behaviour must guide your actions. The future indicates a definite change of direction, so it is important at this time to learn from your responses to the terrible time you have been through, and to find a way of envisaging a future without a repeat of this pain. But it is also important to remain open emotionally and not to become embittered. To achieve this, the best remedy is to embark on a very positive project; try to find a way of doing some good instead of becoming resentful. From your actions towards others now, good things will flow. This forecast is also most powerful in late spring.

43

The moving lines

If any of your throws produced three identical coins (suns or moons), this is called a moving line. Read the relevant line(s) below, then change the line(s) to the opposite symbol, and look up and read the new forecast (see pages 44–5). Don't forget that your tablet of throws is written from the bottom up, so your first throw is the bottom one.

● If your first throw produced three sun coins: don't plunge heedlessly into an attack on someone you feel aggrieved with, or headlong into a difficult situation. First, weigh up the strength of your own position and of your resolve. Be sure of success before you finally commit yourself.

● If your second throw was three sun coins: be ready for anything! A difficult time lies ahead but, if you are ready for this, you will be prepared and you won't be surprised. Keep very calm, act reasonably, and you will come safely through a testing moment.

● If your third throw produced three sun coins: you will have to walk a rather lonely path for a while, but it is better to do this than join forces with someone whose values are abhorrent to you. Being alone means also being distant, and this in turn could cause muttering against you from those who don't understand why you've chosen to act as you do. But in the fullness of time you will be vindicated, and others you value will understand and sympathize with the choices you feel forced to make now.

● If your fourth throw was three sun coins: this is not the moment to strain at the leash and try to escape from your feelings of claustrophobia. Restless as you may feel, difficulties will arise if you attempt to break clear of these constraining forces now. But this may cause you much personal stress and it may be difficult to follow the advice offered here, which is to ride it out without becoming stubborn. If you can put restlessness to one side for a time, all will go well eventually. Can you summon up the necessary patience?

● If your fifth throw produced three sun coins: weeds return even when you uproot them, and so it is with someone causing you personal grief – they return to cause more upset. But don't give up in your determination to be free of this person in the future. Resolution is needed, and resolution will ultimately bring freedom.

○ If your sixth and final throw resulted in three moon coins: you are so close to overcoming your problems, but at this point it is vital to guard against a repeat of these circumstances. With victory in your sights, you must make sure you don't ever lapse back into a state where you allow problems to overwhelm you, like tall weeds choking a beautiful plant. Be alert.

44 Girl in the driving seat

Made up of Wind and Sky, if you are the eldest daughter, or a father, this reading will have greater significance for you, suggesting a moment of key importance is about to occur.

Success comes through a change in the balance of power. The image of this reading is connected with the time just past midsummer, when the balance is changing. The great rush of energy before the Summer Solstice is over and the days are beginning to lengthen – historically, the female energy taking precedence over the male. In the days when these forecasts were originally written it was unthinkable for the female to be more powerful than the male. However, today we can see an alternative vision. There are times when one partner has to assume the greater responsibility, and this may be the person who might normally be more retiring and supportive, historically the female of the couple. Today, of course, this is not unusual: it may well be the mother, being the higher earner, who continues to go out to work while the father provides the all-important home and childcare. Or, if one career has a momentary downturn, the other steps into the breech. This reading suggests this is a time when the other partner takes up the mantle of responsibility, and may even seek new options and opportunities with impunity, because events demand that this must happen. When the pendulum swings towards the normally more supportive partner, and they must take the lead, so be it: fear or self-doubt must not get in the way. If the arrogance of the other partner is not aroused, nor their fragile self-image threatened, all will be well. So, this reading suggests a change in the balance of a relationship (maybe only for a short time) – either of strong/weak, old/young, or male/female – but a true accord and exchange of power occurring between them. From this, much character can be built, and progress and good fortune can be achieved.

44

The moving lines

If any of your throws produced three identical coins (suns or moons), this is called a moving line. Read the relevant line(s) below, then change the line(s) to the opposite symbol, and look up and read the new forecast (see pages 44–5). Don't forget that your tablet of throws is written from the bottom up, so your first throw is the bottom one.

◗ If your first throw produced three moon coins: take the time and trouble to consider whether someone who is in an inferior position to you (perhaps intellectually, if not morally) has gained too much power over your thoughts and ideas. Be ready to stand by your own moral dictates.

● If your second throw resulted in three sun coins: try to put a stop to anyone with bad intentions by gentle diplomacy rather than outright confrontation. Subtle soothing will work best to limit their aggressive behaviour.

● If your third throw produced three sun coins: at all costs, resist pressure to join forces with someone who is behaving cruelly to others. There is a situation developing which may seem to offer interesting possibilities should you fall in with a particular crowd or individual who has strong ideas – but they may not be completely honest. How you judge this, and what path you take, will have serious consequences.

- If your fourth throw resulted in three sun coins: someone of dubious talent is offering some work connection. It would be as well to tolerate this person and meet them part way, as long as doing so doesn't involve behaving badly to others. Simply be aware of this person's limitations.

- If your fifth throw was all sun coins: you must remain true to your own high standards and produce the best possible work – even if you are surrounded by inferior-minded peers or co-workers who would settle for much less. You actually have the power to inspire those less fitted for the job than you to greater heights; as a result, success will be yours!

- If your sixth and last throw gave you three sun coins: ignore the taunts of anyone who is ignorant of your noble aims. You must be guided by your own passion and enthusiasm – both of which tell you what is the best way forward. You are right to remain aloof from someone you wish to have no more to do with. Success lies ahead.

45 All for one and one for all

This forecast, a combination of Earth and Lake, has even greater personal impact if you are either a mother (Earth) and/or the third or younger daughter (Lake). This would signify that you are approaching a key moment in your life.

A forecast full of good omens. This reading depicts a group of people working in close harmony for the good of all – such as might be hoped for in a close family, or a tight community. What is important here is that this group of people have similar and well-integrated philosophical aims, even perhaps a shared spiritual feeling, which ensures that they are speaking a common language to one another, and that their aims have been well thought out, with the best intentions. One clear leader is among the group, and yet this leader is neither arrogant nor at odds with the others. A unity is achieved under the inspiration of this leader that guarantees success – even when there are considerable problems to be dealt with. The wisdom of the group as a whole, and their spokesman, recognizes the need for readiness in any situation. This awareness of the potential for misunderstanding, and that personal woe often results from a failure to see events that are shaping around us, means that as a group there is a greater readiness to be alert to outside events, preventing problems from gaining hold. Confidence in the leader suggests that personal grievances between members of the group will be kept to a minimum. So, success is achieved through co-operation between many for the good of all. Also, one person has the interests of everyone equally at heart, and will work to preserve them. From this combined effort, and from this group dynamic, powerful rewards can be achieved. It is teamwork, and inspirational leadership, that is essential.

45

The moving lines

If any of your throws produced three identical coins (suns or moons), this is called a moving line. Read the relevant line(s) below, then change the line(s) to the opposite symbol, and look up and read the new forecast (see pages 44–5). Don't forget that your tablet of throws is written from the bottom up, so your first throw is the bottom one.

◗ If your first throw was three moon coins: the most important thing to establish from the outset is a firm central person around whom all can rally. Decide carefully, between as many people as are concerned, who should be spokesperson, or who it is you should be led by, and all will come out wonderfully. Without leadership, the path you take would simply meander.

◗ If your second throw was three moon coins: unknown forces are pulling you together with other members of a group for your own good sake. Yield to these influences, for they ensure your progress in an important dream. A great potential for understanding will emerge between you, as long as you are all sincere.

◗ If your third throw produced three moon coins: you may feel left out of a group to which you wish to belong – either concerning friendships or business. But don't be dismayed, for in time, and with honest intention, a way will open. You will find an affinity with the person of central importance to the whole group, and this will ultimately bring you to your goal. But you must always act with sincerity, and never with grumpiness!

● If your fourth throw resulted in three sun coins: you may find yourself the focus of a group's intentions, and it is right that you should accept this responsibility, because you have very honourable intentions concerning the aim of the group rather than a need for personal honours. Everything augurs well, and you are capable of playing this role.

● If your fifth throw resulted in all sun coins: even if there are some people who don't seem to share the aims or wishes of the group as a whole, a good-hearted leader without overweening pride will effect amazing changes. Ultimately, working together on a project dear to most will bring success in an ambition cherished by everyone.

◗ If your last throw resulted in all moon coins: if wish to become close to another person who does not understand your intentions, let your sadness about this be seen. It is not always through seeking sympathy that results are achieved; in fact, very often the opposite is true. However, in this case, your genuine feelings will be appreciated, and the unity you hope for can be achieved after all.

46 To the top of the tree

Being composed of Wind and Earth, this forecast has greater personal significance if you are an eldest sister (Wind) and/or a mother, the Earth.

Success is achieved through seizing the golden moment. The image of this reading is of a tree growing up from the earth and flourishing. The powerful overall meaning is one of success, but just as it takes some time for a tree to grow straight and true, there is also a connection here with time and effort, and the necessary determination and hard work. The main aspect of the reading is of upward growth – complete ascent, someone rising from nothing to a great and powerful position. The effort that may have been undertaken in this rise is significant, but so, too, is the certainty of success. Now is the moment to approach someone who is in a position to realize some of your dreams. You need not be nervous about this, for you have the power to impress and the talent to back up the opportunity. Everything that comes to fruition now comes from modest determination, rather than loud or aggressive attention seeking. This is a golden moment, and all the effort you put into gaining a position, or opening doors to the future, will be well placed. But this is a time to go after a dream, not simply to expect this dream to land on your doorstep! Action is required to achieve a deeply desired goal: it is as though considerable ambition has been marshalled with outstanding results. Much activity is required, and real hard work will be recognized. Travel is likely in pursuit of your goals and, in an almost mystical way, the direction south will be significant. From very modest but repeated actions – like a child practising the violin for just a few minutes, but every day – something great will finally be achieved. Like a tree, it will be necessary to grow in wind and rain, against problems and setbacks; but the rewards will be worth all your efforts.

46

The moving lines

If any of your throws produced three identical coins (suns or moons), this is called a moving line. Read the relevant line(s) below, then change the line(s) to the opposite symbol, and look up and read the new forecast (see pages 44–5). Don't forget that your tablet of throws is written from the bottom up, so your first throw is the bottom one.

◗ If your first throw resulted in three moon coins: knowing which way you want to go, you have the resources to make your first steps towards a powerfully imagined dream. You gather strength from the smallest stimulus, but you have enough steadiness and determination to succeed in this first most important phase: good fortune awaits you.

● If your second throw produced three sun coins: don't judge the sincerity of a person's heart now by their outward and possibly terse manner. What is important is the honesty and goodness of their character. Their approach may be different from your expectations, but their integrity is certain.

● When the third throw produced three sun coins: obstacles that might have been expected will disappear. Thus, a determined effort towards a goal will have some almost divine help, and everything will move along fairly easily towards the end you seek. Use the time wisely and well.

◗ If your fourth throw resulted in three moon coins: genuine ability, and the perfect opportunity afforded by the present moment, ensure the most exceptional achievement and good fortune. There is a promise of fame, in the judgement of gods and men, and a suggestion that such status is deserved, as there is a spiritual element to what is achieved.

◗ If your fifth throw produced three moon coins: there is a reminder here that it takes focus and perseverance to achieve a substantial goal, but by small enduring steps towards an important destination, that end comes closer and closer until you reach it. As each goal is achieved along the route, the test is to stay calm and keep steady in the face of such success. Hurrying will not bring the end nearer, but steady continuous progress guarantees a lasting prize worth attaining.

◗ If your final throw resulted in three moon coins: it is only from careful consideration of what will be required – in terms of strength and training – that you will come through the dark moments that sometimes threaten a worthwhile but demanding goal. If you have this unwavering perseverance, you will emerge victorious into the bright sunshine.

47 Exhaustion

A combination of Water and Lake, this reading has even stronger impact for you if you are either a second son (Water), or a third or younger daughter (Lake). This would signify that a peak moment of importance is approaching.

Success comes through staying calm and believing in yourself. This reading describes a time when your character will be sorely tested. The important thing is to try to remain not only calm, but actually cheerful, for with this smiling determination and good-humoured self belief, a way through many frustrations will be found. At present you appear to be surrounded by small-minded people. In addition, you have an exhausting amount of work to get through, and your efforts seem to be quite unappreciated. But don't let your serenity of mind be undermined by others – you have inner reserves that will carry you through this difficult period, whereas those who are making life hard for you don't have this same reservoir to draw from. For now, external conditions are not in your favour. Frustrations mount, and work outweighs leisure. Anyone you attempt to talk to, to redress the balance, seems unable to understand your worries, or to comprehend the injustice. But a firm belief in yourself will carry you through. Remain centred, find faith within, and don't waste your breath on those people who will only add to your growing sense of frustration. Much of what is affecting you is outside your control, but if you can accept these limitations as philosophically as possible, your balanced approach and cheerful demeanour will be your saving grace. Don't let others get you down with their shallow judgements. Though present circumstances are restrictive, this is not permanent. If you can just bring a smile to your face, every day, you will somehow find the energy you need to cope with these feelings of emotional and spiritual exhaustion.

47

The moving lines

If any of your throws produced three identical coins (suns or moons), this is called a moving line. Read the relevant line(s) below, then change the line(s) to the opposite symbol, and look up and read the new forecast (see pages 44–5). Don't forget that your tablet of throws is written from the bottom up, so your first throw is the bottom one.

◗ If your first throw produced three moon coins: don't give in to total melancholy in a troubling situation, and sit in an empty space meditating on gloom. Only inner strength and determined positive thinking will help you now – further gloomy thoughts will certainly worsen your inner turmoil.

● If your second throw produced three sun coins: even normal everyday life appears oppressive at the moment. If you allow yourself to sink deeper into self-doubt and depression you may fail to recognize a good omen when it arrives, perhaps in the form of a person with the power to help you. The situation is undesirable, but by remaining positive and patient you will get through it.

◗ If your third throw presented three moon coins: even when you're trying to push ahead through difficult times, you come across obstacles that appear to be insurmountable. Don't allow yourself to be defeated by things that shouldn't get the better of you, even though these may seem like the last straw that come to break the camel's back! And be very careful not to lean on people or give in to any indulgences that cannot offer you real support. It's better to stand alone.

● If your fourth throw resulted in three sun coins: help is offered from someone in authority – but it seems very slow in coming. Nevertheless, this is a test of your ability to be patient and stand fast – ultimately, the rescue will arrive and a significant difference will come from it. In the meantime, be brave and hang on in there!

● If your fifth throw produced three sun coins: despite your good intentions and kindness offered for the good of others, this is not enough to get you out of trouble at the moment. You are thwarted from several quarters. However, as time gently passes, things will improve, conditions will change and a return to normality can be expected.

◗ If your final throw produced all moon coins: what is holding you back now? Your difficulties are on their way out, but it seems as if invisible bonds with no real power are still restraining you. Once you realize that there is nothing really holding you back any more, and adjust your views accordingly, your problems will be overcome. At the moment, your troubles are more in your mind than in reality.

48 The well

This forecast is made up of Wind and Water, so the reading has an even greater significance if you are either an eldest daughter (Wind) or a second son (Water). In both cases this would indicate a period of peak importance is ahead.

Success comes from understanding what is of true value. Fashions come and go, but essentially we remain the same, and our needs are as they always were. The well represents our constant need for water as well as our own inner resources – the spirit that maintains us through difficult times. Sometimes we become distracted with fashionable superfluity, but it is our deepest and most essential needs that should be attended to, and should always come first. And so it is now. If you are reading this forecast from a relationship point of view: be sure that anyone to whom you give your heart has the essential spirit that will work well with yours in a lasting commitment. Don't be distracted by initial appearances, but look deep into your lover's heart and soul. If the reading refers to your career: ensure that your job is rich enough to feed mind and spirit, no matter how well paid it may be. If it's your home: before worrying about the decoration, ensure your house is sound and can protect you, bodily and emotionally. Fashion for its own sake won't bring you pleasure in the long run. If you are looking to the future, the forecast concerns the importance of education. You must neither neglect your education, nor use your knowledge as a weapon. Co-operation with others is infinitely preferable to feeling superior to them. Education is vital and should form the basis of your understanding of people and of life. So, the crux of this forecast is to understand that happiness comes from understanding what is of true value. Consider your choices: don't judge anything by its surface value, and put your true needs above what might only be changing fashions.

48

The moving lines

If any of your throws produced three identical coins (suns or moons), this is called a moving line. Read the relevant line(s) below, then change the line(s) to the opposite symbol, and look up and read the new forecast (see pages 44–5). Don't forget that your tablet of throws is written from the bottom up, so your first throw is the bottom one.

◗ If your first throw resulted in three moon coins: this image refers to the mud at the very bottom of a well. The individual needs to move in clear water, not to wander in the lowest, murky waters of life. It is important, now, to have a strong sense of your own self worth – not to become sullied by low thoughts or low self-esteem. Also, be selective about the company you keep.

● If your second throw produced three sun coins: in this image, fish are swimming in the well, and the good clear water is not being used. Thus, it's possible that you have excellent gifts and qualities that you have forgotten, or which are being neglected. Before this becomes a pattern, and you lose your sense of soul, make every effort to recover your talents and start using your creative abilities.

● If your third throw resulted in three sun coins: beautiful clear water is still not being drawn from the well; so it seems as if a good solution to immediate problems is being overlooked. Make certain you recognize the value of good advice when it is right under your nose.

○ If your fourth throw gave you three moon coins: the image for this line shows the well is being repaired with strong stone. So you, too, at this moment, would benefit from putting yourself 'in repair' – rest and recuperation of mind, body and spirit – as good preparation for a sounder future. You might even want to go on an educational course of some kind, and you must not feel selfish if you look to your own needs for a while. What you do now is a foundation for a healthier future life.

● If your fifth throw resulted in three sun coins: here the well is being fed by a clear cool spring. This symbolizes the importance of having a pure – almost sacred – well spring from which to generate new life. So it may be that you should draw inspiration from someone with a good heart and a clear spirit. Read and listen to their words of inspiration, but it is also important actually to follow them – to 'drink' the water.

○ If your final throw produced three moon coins: good fortune comes with this throw. Now, the well is clear and clean and the water can be freely drawn. Whatever you need to draw from, to accomplish a satisfactory life now, is available to you. This may be an individual; or it may be a situation. All is now flowing properly, however, and the needs you have will be 'watered'.

49 A blazing row

A combination of Fire and Lake, this reading will have even greater impact for you if you are either a second daughter (Fire), or a third or younger daughter (Lake). In either case, you are approaching a key moment in your life.

Success comes from accepting the inevitability of change. This forecast suggests there is some form of conflict in your life. During this disturbance, many different opinions will be aired and examined and, as a result, change will follow. Having tried every way of avoiding a confrontation, you will find it is no longer possible. The signs are that a significant transformation in your life is occurring, right now. This is coming about because life has changed and you have moved on. You may feel that you have grown up, or grown in another way; your way of seeing the world may have been altered by some form of enlightenment. In a relationship, you may no longer see your current partner as in step with you, or no longer want to be in the partnership. In career terms, a different course is emerging – a new direction in a totally different field. As a child may grow up and find a way of being that is freer than that of their parents, this change is inevitable. It's likely that an argument will occur as part of the process. Confrontation is inevitable, because two people now come from two completely different standpoints; there is no way of finding any common ground. The best that can be expected is an agreement to disagree: there is a clash of ideologies, a clash of interests, a clash of emotional responses to the world. From this crisis point, a new pattern of life will emerge. Like the changing seasons, this is natural and not to be feared. The only thing we can be sure of in life, after all, is change, and it is often for the best – you just need to go with the flow. This is an absolute dividing line between the past and the future.

49

The moving lines

If any of your throws produced three identical coins (suns or moons), this is called a moving line. Read the relevant line(s) below, then change the line(s) to the opposite symbol, and look up and read the new forecast (see pages 44–5). Don't forget that your tablet of throws is written from the bottom up, so your first throw is the bottom one.

● If your first throw gave you three sun coins: a way around confrontation is still being sought. When all other options have tried and have failed, change must come; but only if there seems no other choice does a true parting of the ways become critical. If and when this stage is reached it is crucial to be very firm and decisive about the best way to break free from the pattern of the past. Don't jump too early, but make sound preparations.

◗ If your second throw resulted in three moon coins: having tried many different approaches to the problems of the past, which result from a clash of needs and views, things are reaching a head. It would be best to achieve a compromise, but if this is rejected or fails to have the desired effect, a completely new cycle must begin. Be prepared for this to have a powerful impact on your life (and possibly that of another), and to bring a great deal of upheaval; but your future will ultimately benefit from this turbulent change. It's important to be ready to face this new future, and to embrace the changes it brings. A half-way remedy is impossible.

● If your third throw gave you three sun coins: as arguments reach a crescendo, and a split seems called for, there will be many who will advise against it. However, what is most important is that this is your decision and yours alone. Also, that you neither rush into a new life without making the necessary arrangements for a smooth transition, nor are too cautious and cling to the past when the time has come to let go. Think deeply on it, and you will reach the right conclusions; then you must act decisively. You will not lose real friends in the long run.

● If your fourth throw gave you three sun coins: your motives for change are valid, not simply a failure to see another point of view. Change is for the best, everything will settle down, and the future will be more peaceful.

● If your fifth throw resulted in three sun coins: you have the support you need from friends or associates, and the changes you initiate will be for the good of many other people besides yourself.

◗ If your final throw produced all moon coins: you will bring about very significant and far-reaching changes around you. Even though some people won't understand why you have acted as you have, they will not be harmed by your actions. Don't be anxious if you don't have full support for your proposed changes right from the start; all will end well if you stay focused and persevere.

50 Full steam ahead

This forecast being made up of Wind and Fire, this reading is particularly important, and indicates a key moment unfolding in your life, if you are either Wind (the eldest daughter) or Fire (the second daughter).

Excellent good fortune! You will be lucky in your current ventures. Everything in your life is bubbling along nicely, and all the ideas you have now are well timed. You have given intelligent thought to your priorities, and proved yourself to be a kind and generous friend. You have achieved a balance in your head and heart between attending to life's necessities and making space for your spiritual drives. You are quite self-sufficient, yet you are not selfish, being aware of the needs of others, too. You are looking for harmony between duty and personal pleasures, and you will find it. Through strong determination you will now succeed. No matter how many obstacles have been in your path to this point, you are now gently overcoming them. There is an implication of further education of some kind, which you may have recently undertaken. You have definitely started to take over your own fate, placing your daily life on a firmer footing. But don't work harder than you need to; good organization will effortlessly give you the progress you are seeking. You will be rewarded for your efforts, and be appreciated by friends and colleagues. There is plenty in the pot to go round! And you will have enough for entertaining. You have pleased the gods, accepting certain limitations but finding a way around others. Truly, good fortune is ahead. This forecast is associated with spring, and it's likely that this is the season in which it will be fulfilled.

The moving lines

If any of your throws produced three identical coins (suns or moons), this is called a moving line. Read the relevant line(s) below, then change the line(s) to the opposite symbol, and look up and read the new forecast (see pages 44–5). Don't forget that your tablet of throws is written from the bottom up, so your first throw is the bottom one.

◑ If your first throw was all moon coins: you have been busy pruning unnecessary dead wood from your life. You will now be free to reorganize your life in the way you prefer – you are not dealing with someone else's past any longer. Don't look back – a spring breeze is blowing!

● If the second throw was all suns: you are achieving some status and being appreciated by people who have influence. Some people are jealous of your success and focus, but they can't stop your progress or change your good fortune. Don't speak too much: keep your ideas to yourself until you have achieved your goal.

● All sun coins in the third throw: a momentary blip: your progress is delayed briefly. Get the materials you need to complete the tasks ahead of you. Take time to research information that will make your job easier to do, but don't rush. Luck may be connected with a rainy day!

● All sun coins in the fourth throw: you may be trying to act too quickly to impress someone, when you are not ready to be tested. Don't take on a responsibility without considering it well, and be prepared to say 'no' to anyone demanding too much too soon. Support yourself with a team of helpers who are really up to the task in hand, but don't allow yourself to be pressured.

◗ A fifth throw with all moon coins: delegate to those who are prepared to do as you ask. Surround yourself with positive, supportive friends, who are willing to let you take the starring role. Persevere and, with good organization and a willingness to listen to sound advice, you will manage your heavy workload.

● All sun coins in your sixth and last throw: this indicates really good fortune for you. You wisely know when to speak and when to listen; and you are secure enough to know when to promote yourself, and when to hold back. You are attracting admiration in the right quarters, and you will get a lucky break. But really, success comes as a result of your own wise actions and ideas. Being positive and cheerful has brought you to a cherished goal.

51 A thunderstorm

This forecast is made up of two Thunder trigrams, so has considerable impact if you are Thunder, the eldest son. As it is a doubling of your element, it is the most significant reading for you of all those containing Thunder.

Success comes through riding the storm with equanimity and inner conviction. You are heading into a thunderstorm – a moment of intense passion and energy. This storm will have a cleansing capacity, washing away dust and releasing pent-up tensions. Its arrival causes shock and fear, but also celebration. Like the eldest son who suddenly comes of age and becomes more powerful than his father, there is a sense of physical change – a new chapter in life, a complete re-energizing that takes away the apathy and hiatus of the past. This may be relevant emotionally, in which case a passionate love affair may be beginning. You could feel fearful as well as excited, but there is real joy ahead. Equally, the image may apply to work or to a new personal direction you are taking; in this case, too, there is apprehension – perhaps real terror – as well as thrilling feelings. However, what has brought you to this moment is an experience of life that should carry you through all your fears. Having experienced pain, or heartache, or loss, you can stare fear in the face with respect, but without submitting to the overwhelming anxieties of the past. In the face of a challenge, you are equal to it. While other people around you may be alarmed or unable to cope, you can find an inner peace and equilibrium to negotiate the tests that come your way. Concentrate on putting your own affairs in order; and maintain that inner serenity that is borne of the knowledge of your own strength. As the storm breaks, you find in it the energy to fall in love with life, and to live with your passions, your heart and your head in harmony. Laughter cleanses the soul, like a thunderclap, and success comes.

51

The moving lines

If any of your throws produced three identical coins (suns or moons), this is called a moving line. Read the relevant line(s) below, then change the line(s) to the opposite symbol, and look up and read the new forecast (see pages 44–5). Don't forget that your tablet of throws is written from the bottom up, so your first throw is the bottom one.

● If your first throw produced three sun coins: a storm that has been brewing is now ready to break. Once the first shock of thunder is felt, laughter follows. Something major is happening around you, which has the power to cause shock and even fear. But after the initial impact has been felt, matters will move from worry to laughter – however hard this is to imagine at first.

◗ If your second throw resulted in three moon coins: there are moments when there is nothing to do but sit out a powerful storm. So it is now, and any effort to resist the storm will be useless. To survive this downpour, try to remove yourself from harm's way as far as possible, retreating somewhere high and dry, looking inwards and finding strength in what is dearest to you. It's likely that you will suffer some setback, but this will not have a lasting effect, and some of what you thought you had lost will return to you in a miraculous way in the future.

◗ If your third throw gave you three moon coins: like the onslaught of a sudden thunderstorm, fate deals out what feels like a terrible shock to your system. The worst effect of this shock would be to go into free fall and spiral out of control completely. Once the initial shock has been faced and embraced, it is vital to remain focused, enabling you to act wisely and make the best from the situation. Action, rather than retreat, is recommended; and this action, with some effort, will help you to overcome the shock. Surviving the blow will prove worthwhile; for there will be plenty of laughter in the long days ahead.

● If your fourth throw produced three sun coins: this is a moment to batten down the hatches while the storm unleashes its worst. Movement – either forward or back – is impossible. Everything feels crippled and chaotic; but still it will pass.

◗ If your fifth throw resulted in three moon coins: several shock waves seem to burst in succession, yet if you can keep your head and stay very calm, losses can be avoided. Above all, don't despair! Stay centred, and be aware of your own inner value: this will bring you through the storm safely in the end.

◗ If your final throw produced three moon coins: don't react to the breaking storm by rushing straight out into the middle of it! The only way to endure this sudden cloudburst is to keep still and quiet long enough to come to your senses, displacing the sense of shock you are experiencing. When your thoughts are collected, you will find a way to sort out the difficulties and minimize the damage.

52 The snowy mountain

This forecast is double Mountain. If you are a Mountain (a third or subsequent, i.e. younger, son) this will be the most influential forecast of all those containing your sign.

Success comes from remaining calm and acting sensibly under stress. This reading concerns the importance of understanding when to lie low and when to speak. You are facing a crucial moment, and how you act is important. Crises can happen even to the strongest and most successful people, but how you handle your problems now is what will determine your future. Know that at this point it is best to stay quiet and ponder the situation until you have decided on the wisest course of action; then, proceed with a plan. The greatest success will come if you can focus on one main issue. This is not a time to let your mind wander, nor to attempt to solve too many problems at once. If you have several things to contend with, break them down and prioritize their importance. Then do one thing, and do it well. Don't be swayed by a crowd of advisors; and if others around you are experiencing chaos, and worrying without thinking, don't let them distract you unnecessarily. Like a mountain bathed in sunshine, but with its peak still capped in snow, this is a time of polarity: one thing may be true, while its opposite is somehow also true. Don't let this confuse you. Act with the knowledge that these contradictory aspects are relevant, and that there is an appropriate way to behave in these circumstances. If you act after deep consideration, you will not make mistakes.

52

The moving lines

If any of your throws produced three identical coins (suns or moons), this is called a moving line. Read the relevant line(s) below, then change the line(s) to the opposite symbol, and look up and read the new forecast (see pages 44–5). Don't forget that your tablet of throws is written from the bottom up, so your first throw is the bottom one.

◗ If all your coins in the first throw were moons: don't act at all without thinking through what is ahead of you. Give no answer to an important question, and don't be hurried. A moment's pause now can guarantee that you will make the best choice shortly. But be ready to persevere with a course of action, once chosen.

◗ If all your coins were moons in the second throw: you are not responsible for the actions of others. Don't try to change someone's mind if it's made up – even if you can see mistakes around the corner. It is more important to be sure of the wisdom of your own choices, and to think sensibly about those. Your heart should not be your advisor!

● If all your coins were suns in the third throw: you are compelled to stay still and wait. Any attempt to insist on changes or solutions just now will threaten the future for everyone concerned. Don't act in anger, or speak when you are in the heat of emotion. Wait for calmness and clarity, and allow the dust to settle.

◗ If the coins of your fourth throw were all moons: your ego has been hurt and you must wait for this feeling to subside. If your pride has been wounded, don't over-react and threaten your future peace and happiness. Think for a little while longer, get your sense of humour back, and this will help you to act with calm integrity.

◗ If your fifth throw produced all moon coins: you may be feeling misunderstood, or even worry that you are being asked to do more than you feel comfortable with. Don't speak out in haste or anger. Speech may be silver but silence, at present, is golden. Go away for a day and collect your thoughts until you can find a way to express your concerns concisely and without unnecessary heat or emotion. Fewer words will bring better results.

● If your last throw resulted in all sun coins: you have already come through a test of your patience. You have held your peace under provocation, and good fortune is now ahead of you. Be resigned to certain changes, but there is no need to dread them.

53 The tree on the hill

This forecast is made up of Mountain and Wind, so has greater importance if you are either Mountain (the third or subsequent son), or Wind (the eldest daughter). In either case this would point to a key moment in your future.

Success comes through giving yourself time to blossom. The image of this reading is of a tree growing peacefully on a hilltop. The hill suggests tranquillity, a new state from which all future development can now flow. By being steady and well earthed, grace of form and serenity of mind are available to you. Like a tree gently blossoming, you are awakening deep responses in the earth around you, allowing you to progress wisely, with room for expansion of thoughts and feelings. It's important not to push things along too fast now. All the issues that concern you most deeply have a momentum of their own. Allow things to develop gradually, be flexible in your approach to life. Nothing should be hurried; there is a natural order for things to unfold; they should not be pushed. A tree that is forced to grow unnaturally fast loses its strength and pliability. If allowed to grow at its own pace, strength is gained, along with the power to absorb the diversity of life and the buffeting winds of fate. This applies to careers, where experience is valued. It is especially true in relationships, where two people need time to discover each other properly. Haste will result in disappointment, misjudgement, or dishonesty. If this resonates with you, allow time to find yourself, to develop fully, to blossom unrestricted. In personal matters, be calm and allow things to take their time. Gentle perseverance will bring you to your goal; progress is being made little by little, all the time. Recognize that your impact on other people, too, may be gradual, but will have a continuing, lasting influence. Your own self-discovery is important, and the knowledge that you can take time to get matters right.

53

The moving lines

If any of your throws produced three identical coins (suns or moons), this is called a moving line. Read the relevant line(s) below, then change the line(s) to the opposite symbol, and look up and read the new forecast (see pages 44–5). Don't forget that your tablet of throws is written from the bottom up, so your first throw is the bottom one.

◗ If your first throw produced three moon coins: in the first steps to find your inner identity and proper direction, you may spend much time alone and suffer an apparent lack of help, even criticism, for the things you do. But by recognizing the difficulties you will be able to take careful steps, allowing for gradual progress; and this in turn brings eventual success.

◗ If your second throw resulted in three moon coins: your initial progress takes you steadily along and, without undue hurry, all fears and doubts are dissipated. In this blossoming time, you also find many true, close friends, and share good times with them. Such generous, true friendships will last the years.

● If your third throw resulted in three sun coins: if you were to rush now this would lead to an unsatisfactory conclusion, like a house built too quickly without good foundations. It may even be dangerous – or at least have frustrating side effects – to motor through your tasks. Most importantly, take care not to let conflicts and arguments arise through hasty behaviour.

If your fourth throw resulted in three moon coins: for a moment, events in life propel you into an uncomfortable position, which is not of your making and not to your liking. However, if you think carefully, speak gently, and avoid hostility of any kind, you will find some kind of safe haven, where you can gain time and sit out the difficulties. To make yourself too loud or too visible would be a mistake at this time!

If your fifth throw brought you three sun coins: you have probably achieved an important ambition, or arrived early at a high point in your career or in personal terms. Jealousy may be a problem around you, and even good friends may judge you with unfair comments. But sensitive behaviour will bring things back on course in time, though it may not happen quickly. In the end, all will be peaceful and happy.

If your final throw produced three sun coins: quite simply, you are destined for greatness, retaining your modesty and having a lasting impact on those around you. Yet this destiny was not achieved through a desire for greatness, but from a true expression of your heart. Good fortune is assured!

54 The new girl

Made up of Lake and Thunder, this forecast has even greater significance for you if you are either a third or subsequent daughter (Lake) or an eldest son (Thunder).

Success will come through tact and subtle behaviour. The image of this reading is of a young woman who has moved into a new situation, in which she has to deal with the position, behaviour and feelings of an older woman. This might be in business, where a younger woman moves to a job where she has to work with a powerful older woman in a senior position. More likely it is a relationship issue – you may have met or married a man who has powerful older women in his life: mother, sister, aunt or friends. If so, you need to behave carefully, with tact and subtlety. Many unspoken emotions simmer below the surface; only through the most perceptive analysis of these unarticulated feelings will you avoid a crisis. It's important to preserve harmony within the family or group dynamic. When affections are involved, it is hard to find an unselfish way of proceeding in relation to the others concerned. If this reading applies to your career, approach the situation with tact and care. Some form of co-operation will be necessary and the chances are that this will be between two sensitive women. Just as the girl who marries a beloved son must find a bond with his mother that recognizes and respects her importance, so you must now look for someone's best qualities. Try not to force an argument; it would be wise to be well-mannered if your emotions are strongly engaged. Only by seeking a working relationship with this woman will you achieve what you want, and some sacrifice may come with this. From the outset, decide whether this would mean giving up too much of yourself. There is no right answer to this question; if you go into the relationship or situation you must do so with your eyes open, accepting the prevailing conditions.

54

The moving lines

If any of your throws produced three identical coins (suns or moons), this is called a moving line. Read the relevant line(s) below, then change the line(s) to the opposite symbol, and look up and read the new forecast (see pages 44–5). Don't forget that your tablet of throws is written from the bottom up, so your first throw is the bottom one.

● If your first throw produced three sun coins: be prepared to accept a position near someone of authority or rank, but to be tactful and a little reserved in the relationship. If you draw too much attention to yourself, you will give offence and perhaps lose the patronage of the person you admire.

● If your second throw produced three sun coins: if there has been a disappointment in love or in a relationship of importance to you, there is no need to lose faith in life or in your own strength and spirit. Always cling to your own inner faith and sense of loyalty to what is dear to you; through this, you will survive the unhappiness and find a new and happier life again in the future.

◗ If your third line was all moon coins: you may be prepared to go into a relationship that will tax your sense of self with a subsequent loss of self-esteem. There may be aspects of the situation that will still be beneficial to you, but you must be prepared to cope with the consequences.

● If your fourth throw resulted in three sun coins: slightly different from the preceding throw, this suggests you have the choice to remain outside a compromising relationship, to find dignity without a lover if necessary. This choice will have a profound outcome, as a stronger, better relationship will bring you happiness down the line.

◗ If your fifth throw produced three moon coins: this image is of someone marrying outside their own life circumstances. There can be beauty and grace in the act of being prepared to forget personal pride or rank, and to live happily in changed circumstances. Partly this is a question of disposition – the power to be flexible and to be free from vanity or conceit.

◗ If your final throw produced three moon coins: this line suggests that there is no real connection between two people in a relationship, and that it was only for appearances that the pairing occurred. In this situation, there is no real happiness in an empty marriage.

55 The midday sun

This forecast is made up of Fire and Thunder, so the reading has greater significance if you are the second daughter (Fire), or the eldest son (Thunder). In either case this would suggest a peak moment is about to unfold in your life.

Success is yours – live in the present! This is an extraordinary symbol: the sun at the height of its powers at midday: a zenith of expression has been reached. You are now in a time of magnificent abundance. It takes one with an extraordinary vision, and a hugely motivated personality, to achieve what you have done. This is a cause for celebration, a time to rejoice in the abundance that has come your way. Like the most perfect summer day in a country (like England!) where such days are not the norm, there is a feeling of great joy and exhilaration at its arrival. This flowering of achievement may spread into all areas of your life: in creative terms, in personal terms, in achieving a serious ambition. Many people will bask in the sunshine beside you; you can spread warmth and hope to others. It is, of course, important to remember that such perfection does not last forever; but this should not detract from the celebration of reaching such a moment and living it to the full. An awareness of the passing of time is not a cause for sadness, just a reminder to recognize the moment, live fully in the present and make the most of it. This is a time of great clarity: the ideal time to deal with business affairs and contracts, write books, or carry out any legal business. This brilliant clarity shines like a beacon into areas that were previously difficult to comprehend; your brain is razor sharp and logic will win the day. Like a party on Midsummer Day, tomorrow may be fractionally shorter, and the hospitality a little less. But the crucial thing is to seize the moment, not to look anxiously into the future. Such magnificence has been achieved that nothing but joy should come from it.

55

The moving lines

If any of your throws produced three identical coins (suns or moons), this is called a moving line. Read the relevant line(s) below, then change the line(s) to the opposite symbol, and look up and read the new forecast (see pages 44–5). Don't forget that your tablet of throws is written from the bottom up, so your first throw is the bottom one.

● If your first throw produced three sun coins: the time is ripe for a meeting between one person with exceptional clarity of mind and another with great force of character. You should recognize yourself in one character or the other; and from this, extraordinary achievements will flow.

◗ If your second throw resulted in three moon coins: good intentions and exceptional vision may be clouded temporarily by people who seem to be working against you rather than with you. But dedication to the truth – without any prima donna behaviour – will finally win through, and common sense will prevail. Allow some time for an apparent miracle to work!

● If your third throw was all sun coins: you are momentarily prevented from acting wisely, in the way that you wish to; but this situation will not last. Wait for matters to settle down, and for several people who currently disagree around you to exhaust themselves.

● If your fourth throw resulted in three sun coins: all frustrations seem to melt away in a moment of blinding light and clarity. You meet a soul mate, someone of great intelligence and a good heart. Working together, you will revolutionize the existing way of doing things, guaranteeing great success.

◗ If your fifth throw resulted in three moon coins: you impress someone at the top of their game who can help you, in turn, to achieve your ambitions. This is achieved through modesty on your part, also clarity and excellence focus. Many blessings unfold for everyone concerned – fame, fortune, friends, and joy.

◗ If your final throw produced three moon coins: don't allow yourself to become arrogant, even though you have attained so much and become rightly celebrated for your contributions and achievements. Consider which goals are really important to you, and be sure you're not in the process of getting almost the opposite of what you would wish. It's important to remain accessible and to stay in touch with people.

56 The traveller

This forecast is made up of Mountain and Fire, so the reading has greater significance if you are either a third or subsequent son (Mountain), or a second daughter (Fire). In either case this is likely to be a key moment for you.

Success comes from feeling your way with care. This reading describes the moment when we are in a strange landscape – like foreigners, having to learn our way around places with which we are unfamiliar. What is significant about such a moment is that we behave with less arrogance, are more hesitant, needing to feel our way along. The people with whom we come into contact are different, and we cannot automatically assume that we know how they will behave, or react, to the things we do. We may take the trouble to be more cautious and polite. And so it is now: this is a time for caution and politeness, for behaving as though we were guests in another person's land. Being well mannered and alert to the subtlest feelings of others, we can win approval, have a good experience, and make important new friends. There is a situation that demands cautious behaviour, tact and politeness. Like someone travelling through unknown lands, be observant, take care to associate with people who are helpful, and be appreciative of the warmth you are shown. For a while, you may feel that you have no true home; you may feel distant from other people, cut off from those who are normally close, or forced onto your own resources. No one can reach you, or feel as you feel; but this is not permanent. Nothing will last, so make temporary arrangements, as you do when you travel. A short rental, a short-term work contract, or even a whirlwind love affair. The moment is apt for a swift set of events, not a prolonged state of affairs. There may even be some dealings with the law; which must be settled quickly. Good fortune is assured if events are concluded quickly.

56

The moving lines

If any of your throws produced three identical coins (suns or moons), this is called a moving line. Read the relevant line(s) below, then change the line(s) to the opposite symbol, and look up and read the new forecast (see pages 44–5). Don't forget that your tablet of throws is written from the bottom up, so your first throw is the bottom one.

○ If your first throw produced three moon coins: keep only very positive and good company now. In your present state, where everything is transient, you must not be influenced by negative or unsettling acquaintances. Stay positive, and keep your inner sense of self-worth.

○ If your second throw produced three moon coins: you may be tested many times to see how adaptable you can be in a short-lived situation. Be calm and clear, unassuming and sensitive. You will win help and friendship in unexpected places.

● If your third throw resulted in three sun coins: don't be high-handed or short-tempered now. You are not on the strongest ground, and may be in unfamiliar circumstances. On this occasion, if you try to bluff your way through it will go against you. Don't get embroiled in other people's affairs!

● If your fourth throw produced three sun coins: be on your guard against anyone whose appearance may not be as it seems. This is a moment when you may not be able to relax, but may feel as though you are on unfamiliar ground.

◗ If your fifth throw produced three moon coins: this indicates a smoothing of the ways, and luck in foreign places. A road takes you away from what has been familiar, but it's the right road to travel and leads to a new life in a different place. A new circle of friends and a more adventurous lifestyle are omens of good things to come. This throw shows you are falling on your feet.

● If your sixth and final throw resulted in three sun coins: you are still in a strange landscape that demands you learn its ways. Beware of careless words or behaviour – you will regret them in the near future. Laughter and your social life must not get in the way of your real needs: take care of the basics before you rest.

57 A gentle breeze

This forecast is double Wind, so its impact is significant if you are an eldest daughter, in which case it is the most important forecast containing Wind that you could throw. This indicates that a key moment in your life is unfolding.

Success will come through moving gently towards your goal. Your greatest powers of understanding are required now. Wind is the element of discovery, penetrating through the cracks and crevices of the structured world, gusting ships across the seas to new places, causing change and stirring energy. Its presence is strong and always felt – even the gentlest summer breeze that cools a cheek on a hot day. The wind wafts the clouds and brings the rain; the sky is then cleansed and refreshed, and left clear and calm afterwards. This serenity and clarity is what you must seek now. Demands will be made on your judgement: you must achieve clarity of purpose and be bold enough to discover what is as yet unknown to you. To stay still would be a mistake; like the wind, you must keep moving. Rays of light penetrate the darkest corners and bring radiance, and wind can find a chink in the door when all else seems secure. In such a restless way, you must move onwards now, like a summer wind. Whatever your goal, it will be achieved through gentle persistence. It's important to feel the gentle breath of the wind on your own back, urging you forward to meet new people and new situations. Nothing is gained by force; but if you have a well-defined goal, a clear objective and keen powers of judgement, the smallest steps will carry you gradually over a great distance. Now is the moment to voice your ideas and desires, addressing them softly to the summer breeze and sending them out to the universe. Travel is essential. too, and your aims will be realized by pursuing one course without letting up. Put your thoughts into action.

57

The moving lines

If any of your throws produced three identical coins (suns or moons), this is called a moving line. Read the relevant line(s) below, then change the line(s) to the opposite symbol, and look up and read the new forecast (see pages 44–5). Don't forget that your tablet of throws is written from the bottom up, so your first throw is the bottom one.

◗ If your first throw produced three moon coins: the moment is characterized by a lack of determination about where you are heading. Don't let doubts cloud your judgement and, most importantly, avoid indecision – it will send you off in too many different directions. Make one choice, and stick with it.

● If your second throw produced three sun coins: you must confront someone who is undermining you by suggestion and implication. Look into this carefully and find out the source of this gossip. If you can identify the source of this trouble and bring it out into the open, all the power of this person will disintegrate. There is no substance to these claims, even though they are unsettling you.

● If your third throw produced three sun coins: as with the first throw, it is essential to be decisive and to act firmly. Any lingering hesitation about what to do will be damaging and cause you problems for the future. There's no need to weigh up the issues perpetually: consider your options, and then act.

If your fourth throw resulted in three moon coins: you have an opportunity now to move everything forward. Your actions are modest but fruitful; a good combination of gentleness and energy. Able to satisfy many demands, your ventures now seem especially successful.

If your fifth throw gave you three sun coins: you may have inherited circumstances which were difficult at first; but now a new path emerges, and a way though the obstacles can be seen. Changes are for the better, and a new method of working, or a different approach to work, will help you overcome problems from the past. Good fortune comes gradually.

If your final throw produced three sun coins: although you can trace the source of rumours and trouble, and know who may be making your life difficult, it may be wiser to retreat rather than to pursue this enemy at present. You may come across unexpected danger if you try to uncover your adversary. Tread carefully!

58 Lake reflects summer

This forecast is made up of double Lake. If you are the third (or younger) daughter (Lake), this reading is especially important for you, and it can be seen to signal the approach of a particularly significant moment for you.

Success comes through a quality of inner strength. Strength can be an internal quality that manifests externally as gentleness; when you have inner strength you can afford to be gentle with others. The lake is deep and reflective, but it exudes serenity. This image of the lake is one of joyfulness and beauty. Such beauty and joy carries others along in its path, so they too feel this mood of happiness. So, if you have truth and serenity in your heart, you can be gentle with people socially, attracting good feelings and joy to you in all relationships. Friendliness will help you to achieve many of your goals and needs; there is no need to intimidate anyone, or to coerce them. Friends offer you advice, support, strength and practical help. At this time, you will acquire deeper knowledge and find other people willing to move mountains to help you. All your work and chores are shared, and become lighter to do. Your influence is powerful, and your popularity grows. So if there is an occasion when you need to appear docile and co-operative, know that you can do this by staying firm within. It's important now to persevere with your wishes, and to exude an inner joyousness for the world to see. Your positive and sunny state of being will affect everyone around you. Be an example to others and lead them through any crises. No matter how much there is to get through, you will bring yourself and others through it without any feelings of drudgery. There is room for discussion, which will yield significant results. After much consideration, a good way to achieve an important goal will be found, with a highly successful outcome. Better still, joy abounds everywhere.

58

The moving lines

If any of your throws produced three identical coins (suns or moons), this is called a moving line. Read the relevant line(s) below, then change the line(s) to the opposite symbol, and look up and read the new forecast (see pages 44–5). Don't forget that your tablet of throws is written from the bottom up, so your first throw is the bottom one.

● If your first throw produced three sun coins: you have an instinct for joy and positive thinking, which will bring you through any tests. In quiet moments you can see deeply into emotional matters and understand what is important for your happiness. Good fortune comes to you partly because your sense of self is beyond petty ego or the dislike of others; in your heart you find serenity and purpose.

● If your second throw resulted in three sun coins: there is cause for joy and celebration. You have found friends who are at your level of high intelligence and sensitivity. All temptations and distractions can be set aside, and you can find happiness and personal fulfilment without envy or frustration.

◗ If your third throw was three moon coins: the challenge of this moment is to rediscover the spring of joy within you. Outside pleasures will not bring you happiness if your inner self feels barren or cold. Look inwards.

● If your fourth throw produced three sun coins: work at full stretch now towards the highest achievement you can. Setting smaller goals will ultimately make you feel denied and cheated. Raise your efforts, now, to their highest levels.

● If your fifth throw resulted in three sun coins: your discernment will be tested now, when you find yourself approached by someone you would do well to ignore. Don't become entangled in affairs with dangerous thinkers. You will remain unharmed and worry free if you understand the potential implications and avoid them.

◗ If your final throw resulted in three moon coins: give in to pleasure by all means, as long as you are sure of yourself within and don't look to expensive luxuries and designer labels to define who you are.

59 Wind rippling the sea

This forecast is made up of Water and Wind, so if you are a second son (Water) or an eldest daughter (Wind), you will find even greater impact from this reading. It suggests that a really significant moment is approaching in your life.

Success comes through a flexible attitude to others. Here, there is a problem of prejudice or arrogance based on ego; in this case someone's ego is threatening your happiness or even stability. In the image, the calm and implacability of the sea is disturbed by the wind blowing over its impenetrable top. So it must be now: either you find yourself compelled to coerce an arrogant person out of their mood of stubborn and egotistical ill will, or you must relax your own egotistical stance towards another person. Co-operation is essential; there is no room for conceit or surly attitudes to others. If a wedge is driven between you and another person, things will fall apart. Only by finding and creating unity will success be ensured, either in business or in relationships. It is vital to meet others half way, and not to object to another's ideas without first considering them. The most damaging emotion now would be jealousy or hard-heartedness; any rigidity will result in the failure of an aim or project – or even a relationship. A flexible attitude towards others, and in particular to their way of thinking, is crucial. Greed, selfishness or superiority would soon lead to deep unhappiness. Knowing how to apply this philosophy under the current circumstances may require a bit of meditation and soul searching. To know exactly how you must behave, and what you must do for and with other people, you must think deeply and decide how they affect you. Be prepared to change your own position, or to tease another intransigent person gently out of their determination to be right in everything. Humility from everyone is required in this situation.

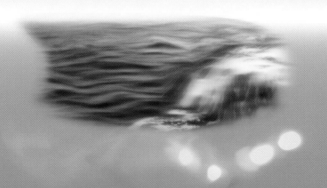

59

The moving lines

If any of your throws produced three identical coins (suns or moons), this is called a moving line. Read the relevant line(s) below, then change the line(s) to the opposite symbol, and look up and read the new forecast (see pages 44–5). Don't forget that your tablet of throws is written from the bottom up, so your first throw is the bottom one.

◗ If your first throw resulted in three moon coins: it's essential that you take time to sort out any differences of opinion right at the outset of a venture or project with other people. Smooth over any feelings of disunity and create harmony amongst all the people involved. Misunderstandings must be cleared up now.

● If your second throw produced three sun coins: if, after embarking on a scheme involving other people, you find yourself feeling anxious about these people, you must work hard now to rationalize your difficulties and get over them. Ill humour or clashes of temperament will cause ongoing problems, so solve all disagreements now.

◗ If your third throw gave you three moon coins: enormous personal strength is needed for you to get through a period of intense work. Only by setting aside personal desires and working towards this goal relatively selflessly will you come through it. If you can distance yourself from outside demands and do what is required, you will be very successful – but ego must play no part in it.

◗ If your fourth throw produced three moon coins: you must work alongside others at this time to achieve an important goal, but you must put aside personal ambitions and friendships and work for the good of everyone. If you can remove self-interest from the equation, your desire for achievement will be completely successful.

● If your fifth throw resulted in three sun coins: your own clever and creative ideas may overcome a stalemate now – either in a relationship, or in an important work venture. A fresh idea is required, and you have the talent and ability to develop one.

● If your sixth and final throw gives you three sun coins: your quick thinking is likely to rescue a difficult situation for many close to you. You understand the dangers for someone close, and you are able to overcome them.

60 Overspending

Made up of Lake and Water, this reading will have a greater impact if you are a third or subsequent daughter (Lake) or a second son (Water). In both cases this would suggest you are approaching a moment of key importance in your life.

Success comes from living within your means. This forecast stresses the importance of moderation. It's important now to set limits to what you plan to commit yourself to, and live within those limits. Without boundaries you may become over-burdened and find yourself stretched to danger point – financially, physically, or even emotionally. This might happen in several ways, so it would pay you to be moderate in your outlays of time, emotion, money, and even loyalty. Sometimes setting limits can seem negative and confining, but in this situation the limits you impose can be very productive. It's a matter of being economical in a number of ways. By reducing your workload, or working within one specified area, you will have enough energy and resources to do the job well. Imagine you are throwing a banquet for six people rather than a frugal supper for ten; you can put aside the perfect amount of time and resources to carry this off really well. No matter how persuasive others may be, stay within your means. No one will think badly of you, but if you attempt more and fail, you will lose face. This is a time for belt-tightening and penny-pinching, and the same goes for your time and energy. Be sensible on your own behalf, and don't ask more of yourself than you can reasonably give. Look at every area of your life: often, illness comes from overwork and over-expenditure, so it is likely that the effects from one form of excess may spill into another. Be very honest and ask yourself if you have taken on too much. If you can see that you have done so, make changes at once, and cut down your load. Success comes from working sensibly within your limits.

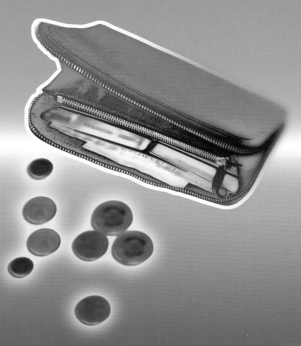

The moving lines

If any of your throws produced three identical coins (suns or moons), this is called a moving line. Read the relevant line(s) below, then change the line(s) to the opposite symbol, and look up and read the new forecast (see pages 44–5). Don't forget that your tablet of throws is written from the bottom up, so your first throw is the bottom one.

● If your first throw produced three sun coins: recognize the moment. You may be really determined to embark on several demanding projects, but to do so now will cause you distress, and you are likely to find limitations imposed on you from outside. Take on only as much as you know you can manage well.

● If your second throw resulted in three sun coins: it's important, despite all the advice offered by the main part of this reading, to take advantage of an opportunity to act when it does arise. Assuming sensible limits have been set for achieving goals and making certain commitments, don't lose this moment for action. You may miss an opportunity if you don't act at once.

◗ If your third throw resulted in three moon coins: this is definitely not a time for extravagance. Put all areas of your life on a budget now, and be ready to organize a regime you feel you can live within. This might be in the area of diet, health, finance or work, but in whichever case it's important to be organized and efficient.

If your fourth throw produced three moon coins: for true happiness, you must find a balance between imposed limits that feel natural and are relatively easy to follow, and those more punitive limits that cause distress and are impossible to stick to. For instance, follow a healthy diet without too much excess, but don't try to live on too little, as it will involve too much effort and self-denial. This reading is about limitation and moderation, not starvation!

If your fifth throw gave you three sun coins: don't ask other people to suffer restrictions that you wouldn't accept yourself. If you see that cutbacks and restraint are necessary, lead by example. This will ensure there is a happy and successful outcome for everyone.

If your sixth and last throw produced three moon coins: be sensible in the parameters you set, but don't deny yourself or others everything. It is wise to be moderate now, but not too ascetic.

61 The sailing boat

This forecast is a combination of Lake and Wind. If you are a third or subsequent daughter (Lake), or an eldest daughter (Wind), this forecast will have a greater impact for you, suggesting a key moment in your life is approaching.

A gentle and subtle approach will lead to success. The image here is of wind ruffling the surface of the water and filling a sail. Its message is that you can make progress now by influencing someone who may be difficult, but it depends on how you approach them. Wind is invisible, yet its effects are clear: the boat makes swift progress once the sails are filled. Conditions are perfect for a mutual confidence that will allow the successful fulfilling of ambitions, but that influence must be subtle. You need to understand the other person, to get close to them and into their confidence, just as the wind is close to the water and to the sail. Then, this other person will listen to you, which will make a difference to the way they think and act. Your instincts are good, and you are forceful and true; you need to whisper your thoughts gently to this person just as the wind whispers to the sea and the boat. If you can achieve this, no matter how impossible it may seem, you will achieve extraordinary results. Travel may be crucial to finalize details and drive home your victory. But throughout, you must be free of prejudice and true to yourself. You should be content to carry out the wishes of someone in charge, or to whom you are responsible; you should also enjoy being gently persuasive with those who are dependent on you, or look up to you. This can be a time of mutual productivity and good communication. Your clarity and honesty will speak eloquently, and your subtlety in understanding the person you need to persuade will ensure your success. You will be rewarded if you can find a way to achieve your goal without conflict.

61

The moving lines

If any of your throws produced three identical coins (suns or moons), this is called a moving line. Read the relevant line(s) below, then change the line(s) to the opposite symbol, and look up and read the new forecast (see pages 44–5). Don't forget that your tablet of throws is written from the bottom up, so your first throw is the bottom one.

● If your first throw produced three sun coins: it's important to be prepared for something challenging now, to be aware that what you do or wish to do will be examined very closely. Expect an explanation, but also be independent and try not to rely on others. It's best to avoid being secretive with anyone for the present.

● If your second throw produced three sun coins: so strong are the feelings in your heart that you will find a close tie with one or more kindred spirits. You have a perceptible influence over others now, but that influence may be unintentional. Use your charisma and powerful character to make a positive difference where it will be of great help. And don't be surprised if the effects of your actions spread and are felt far and wide.

◐ If your third throw resulted in three moon coins: your own happiness seems to depend on others at the moment, because you have allowed this to be so. As a result you may feel extreme joy and happiness, or the sadness and pain of desperation. Yet whether you feel happy or sad is up to you. You must be aware that you lay yourself open to both as long as you are as emotionally open with others as you are at the moment.

◗ If your fourth throw resulted in three moon coins: there is a testing moment ahead, when you must not let others bring you down, and must find enlightenment from someone you respect as wise. Once you have found some true self-belief, be ready to walk unwaveringly along your path. Inner strength will carry you to your goal.

● If your fifth throw produced three sun coins: you must hold several disparate parties together through the power of your own personality. There is potential for arguments and disagreements, but if you stand firm, you can unite many different views.

● If your final throw gave you three sun coins: don't count on words alone to sway someone close to you; actions will have a more profound impact over time.

62 Bird with a message

A combination of Mountain and Thunder, this reading will have greater significance if you are the third or younger son (Mountain), or the eldest son (Thunder). In either case, you are likely to be approaching a key moment in your future.

Simple, unpretentious actions bring good fortune. This reading suggests you will need all your powers to deal with a problem from the world at large. This is a time for those who usually lack power or recognition to be successful. It's essential that you understand the limitations of the moment, however; it would not be in your best interest to push ahead with really significant plans, but it's a good time to press on with smaller ones. Be modest, both in your outward actions and in what you attempt to achieve. Break down larger chores and get through life's little events one day at a time. If you are conscientious and attentive to detail, you will certainly succeed. You don't have vast reservoirs of strength to call upon – neither personal strength, nor strength in numbers. It's important to think deeply about what is possible, and be sensible in what you set out to achieve. Going after lofty dreams would be a waste of strength and imagination; but going after plausible dreams will bear fruit. One image of this reading is of a bird with a message, inspired and soaring into heaven. But the bird cannot fly above the sun; and you, too, should recognize the heights you can attain, and do so joyfully. Be strong, purposeful and confident. It would be most effective at this time to concentrate on all the little jobs that can pile up. There is pleasure and a huge sense of achievement to be gained in tidying up these small affairs. You are in the process of finding a perfect balance between confident self worth and appropriate humility. Finding this balance, you will discover joy and a new lightness of being. Put more serious matters aside while you experience this extraordinary equilibrium.

62

The moving lines

If any of your throws produced three identical coins (suns or moons), this is called a moving line. Read the relevant line(s) below, then change the line(s) to the opposite symbol, and look up and read the new forecast (see pages 44–5). Don't forget that your tablet of throws is written from the bottom up, so your first throw is the bottom one.

◗ If your first throw gave you three moon coins: if a fledgling bird flies from the nest too soon, it may well find itself in danger. At the moment you, too, should be moderate in what you set out to achieve. This is not the time to embark on brave – and possibly foolish – adventures.

◗ If your second throw produced three moon coins: there are times when it's appropriate to find a new way of tackling a problem, and this means breaking with established rules of etiquette. At this moment, it is favourable to find a new way of achieving a desired goal – provided you can do so without losing your sense of honour.

● If your third throw produced three sun coins: this is an important moment in which to exercise excellent judgement concerning trust and commitments. Look ahead at what is required of you, consider any potential hazards and conflicts of interest with others, and try to pay close attention to details which will help you understand the whole picture – then act wisely.

● If your fourth throw was all sun coins: it's not going to be possible to actively pursue a goal at this time; however, you should be ready for a time when that will be possible, so prepare your ideas and strategy for that future day.

◖ If your fifth throw produced three moon coins: take advice from someone who is retired or no longer offers professional guidance. There are confusing signs in your work and personal life now, and only someone who is completely unconcerned in them can help you decide how to proceed.

◖ When your last throw resulted in three moon coins: once you have achieved something worthwhile, it's important to know when to stop. The more you push yourself, the more danger you expose yourself to. Excessive activity would be dangerous at this time, so you must exercise caution in what you take on.

63 The boiling kettle

This forecast is made up of Fire and Water, so the reading has greater impact if you are the second daughter (Fire), or the second son (Water). In either case, this suggests a moment of peak importance is unfolding in your life now.

Success comes from staying ahead of the game. In this forecast, the balance of moons and suns in the pictorial tablet is in perfect harmony. This is extremely promising, suggesting a moment of peak prosperity, a time of balance and proportion. However, at this time we must look ahead to see that events will need adjusting. A continuation of the state of affairs that has brought us to this point would cause the situation to overheat – if a kettle boils for too long, the water will all evaporate. In other words, everything up to now is right and for the best; but caution is required to understand how to go forward. So, congratulations are in order as you have come to a moment of perfection; you have been both industrious and intelligent in your use of time, and everything you have done has been well planned and apt. Old has given way to new, and a change has been created to good effect. Now, a new strategy is in order – you must keep ahead of the trend. Success seems close, and so it is, but only with a good plan for the future. Don't lapse into arrogance, and remain grateful for the circumstances that have brought you this far. Indifference would be disastrous, now, so stay on your toes, think creatively, be alert to the need for a change of approach in order to prolong your success. If you can grasp this, you will succeed. And make sure you retain firm control of the future direction you take. This set of circumstances is akin to the approach of autumn – the successful harvest has been brought in, but equally, it's important to know how to prepare for winter. The right activity at the right moment creates order and security.

63

The moving lines

If any of your throws produced three identical coins (suns or moons), this is called a moving line. Read the relevant line(s) below, then change the line(s) to the opposite symbol, and look up and read the new forecast (see pages 44–5). Don't forget that your tablet of throws is written from the bottom up, so your first throw is the bottom one.

● If your first throw resulted in three sun coins: everything drives you forward at the moment – especially pressures from outside; but you are aware of the need for caution in the face of all this excitement, and your own behaviour is measured. This will ensure your success.

◐ If your second throw gave you three moon coins: it's a waste of time to seek accolades now. The work you have done, and the position you have attained, will bring you attention; but success is assured if it is the work, and not the fame, that drives you. This assures happiness and also maintains a sense of personal proportion. Other merits will then come without seeking them.

● If your third throw was three sun coins: you may have struggles ahead to ensure that you hold onto, and develop, the achievements you have begun. However, be careful not to work with people who are unworthy simply as part of your enterprise of expansion. Make sure that like-minded souls, with good hearts, are involved in your projects and future direction.

○ If your fourth throw resulted in three moon coins: no matter how well things are going now, be aware that attention to detail is still a necessity for a continuation of this success and harmony in the future.

● If your fifth throw resulted in three sun coins: hollow gestures won't bring you luck or happiness now. Actions motivated by material greed will ultimately be a mixed blessing. Small gestures of generosity, given with feeling, will be better for both parties than lavish gifts that will not move the recipient as truly. In spiritual matters, small gestures acted out in good faith, and with a true heart, will make a profound impact, whereas grand gestures that are purely ceremonial would have no impact at all.

○ If your final throw produced all moon coins: now you can move forward, away from the past, without looking back. Don't stop to relive perilous moments, or to witness other difficult events, for fear of becoming embroiled. Move on, and away from trouble.

64 First signs of spring

This forecast is made up of Water and Fire, so if you are either the second son (Water), or the second daughter (Fire), this reading will have an even greater impact for you.

Good times ahead, but tread carefully. This moment anticipates the move from winter towards spring: changes are in the air, even though they are not yet with us. As in winter, conditions in your life may still be difficult. There is so much still to be done: too many tasks that never seem to be completed. You have a huge number of responsibilities now – like the time around Christmas with its endless preparations. And, though after Christmas there are more grey, cold days to come, the light is returning. So it is now: you have work and responsibilities which can't be shared, and your desk is piled high; but warmer, lighter, days are truly ahead. You need to sense a tiny source of new energy burning within, which will light your way forwards. At this testing moment, when you have nearly come safely through hard times, you need to speak with caution, move with care, like someone walking along an icy road on a dark day. Tread carefully, and take your time. But don't be despondent, and don't feel unappreciated. Quite suddenly, you will see the shoots of spring bulbs and the first blossom on the trees. Change is happening apace, and some progress can be made now; winter – and it may have been a harsh one – is virtually behind you. The first shoots and blossoming trees indicate that there is new life ahead, even when the days still feel cold. There is hope: after a period of making a constant effort just to survive, there are signs of joy ahead. The tiny new flowers of spring bring expectancy; you feel rejuvenated, regaining vitality and optimism. However hard it gets, life is always worth living, and there is always a moment when new buds appear on seemingly bare trees. A few more steps will take you to them.

64

The moving lines

If any of your throws produced three identical coins (suns or moons), this is called a moving line. Read the relevant line(s) below, then change the line(s) to the opposite symbol, and look up and read the new forecast (see pages 44–5). Don't forget that your tablet of throws is written from the bottom up, so your first throw is the bottom one.

◗ If your first throw produced three moon coins: don't be premature in what you set out to do. The time is still not quite right. If you jump in too early, you will not succeed.

● If your second throw gave you three sun coins: now is the time to make preparations for a trip; however, it is not quite time to set out. Everything – every detail – must first be in order. Learn thoroughly what you need to do to make a proper impression.

◗ If your third throw produced three moon coins: you have a real desire to accomplish an important personal goal, but you need to revise your plans for undertaking this dream. Make it a reality, but do so with careful thought as to whom you need to approach to help you. You need to make a trip.

● If your fourth throw resulted in three sun coins: now, the sun comes out to warm a chilly day. There is a great deal to get through, but your aims are good, and your intentions right. As long as you have the physical stamina to see it through, you will be very successful. Rewards will accrue from this adventure for three years. But be sure you have the strength to take on such a challenging task.

◗ If your fifth throw gave you three moon coins: a new dawn has broken for an entirely new life. Everything proper has been done, you have found the right people to help you, and you have proved you have the staying power to achieve your desires. Victory is achieved, and with it comes a true sense of pride and pleasure. This is all the more true for its contrast with the difficult times you have endured. Good fortune is yours.

● If your sixth and final throw resulted in three sun coins: gather your friends together and celebrate. Spring has arrived, with blossoms to scent the air – it's time to get together with those you love. However, be wary of overdoing it: there is still a lot of work to get through in order to continue in the prosperous vein of this new life. You are celebrating a beginning, not an ending!

Acknowledgements

Writing this book has had a profound effect on me, asking me to think deeply about my own life and what is important. It has unearthed a few surprises! So, my thanks to King Wen, and Confucius, and all the scholars who have contributed to the making of, and understanding of, this amazing treatise. Special thanks to P, for standing by me when the going got very tough. To Quadrille for beautiful books; and to Richard, whose artwork is vibrant and a worthy part of such exquisite philosophy. Thanks to Jim for his clean design, and to Ian, Clare and Fiona, for their work in making the book known. Sabine, your smile makes a visit to Charing Cross Road more worthwhile. Huge thanks to Sian at Waterstones, and to Neil at Dolphin Square. Also, big hugs to everyone at the Adyar Bookshop in Sydney, who sent me a copy – from Oz to England – of Wilhelm's I Ching as a 'thank you' for a book shop talk I gave there one night a few years ago. My first Ching, translated by John Blofeld, was also bought from that shop, so many long years ago. And thanks to my sister Wendy, for asking me to challenge my ideas about making the I Ching modern: hereafter, I dub you the Superior Woman!

Also by Titania Hardie

Hocus Pocus: Titania's Book of Spells
Bewitched: Titania's Book of Love Spells
Titania's Oraqle: A Unique Way to Predict your Future
Enchanted: Titania's Book of White Magic
Titania's Wishing Spells: Health, Wealth, Love, Happiness, Peace, Harmony
Titania's Spell Cards: Love & Success, Health & Happiness, Peace & Harmony
Zillionz: Titania's Book of Numerology
Titania's Fortune Cards
White Magic: Titania's Complete Book of Spells
Witch in the Kitchen: Titania's Book of Magical Feasts
Love Potions: Titania's Book of Romantic Elixirs
Titania's Book of Hours: A Celebration of the Witch's Year
Titania's Star Tarot

First published in 2004 by Quadrille Publishing Ltd
Alhambra House, 27–31 Charing Cross Road,
London WC2H OLS
Reprinted in 2006 for the US

Project editor Anne Furniss
Design and layout Jim Smith
Illustrations Richard Rockwood
Production Beverley Richardson, Vincent Smith

© **Text** Titania Hardie 2004
© **Illustrations** Richard Rockwood 2004
© **Design and layout** Quadrille Publishing Ltd 2004

British Library Cataloguing in Publication Data
A catalogue record for this book is available from the British Library

ISBN-13: 978 184400 122 4
ISBN-10: 1 84400 122 9
Printed and bound in China

10 9 8 7 6 5 4 3 2